CW01021128

Text Colin Greenland
Architectural Text David Lucas

POMEGRANATE ARTBOOKS • SAN FRANCISCO

Published by Pomegranate Artbooks
in association with Curved Space UK Ltd.
and Incredible Images, Inc. 1993

Pomegranate Artbooks
Box 6099
Rohnert Park, California 94927

Originally published in Great Britain by Paper Tiger, an imprint of Dragon's World Ltd.

Designed by Roger Dean and Martyn Dean

ISBN 1-56640-449-5

Printed in Hong Kong

The War of the Worlds series of paintings was designed by Roger Dean and painted by:
Tim White, pages 104/105, 106, 107, 108, 111, 118/119
Richard Clifton-Dey, pages 112/113, 114/115, 116/117, 120/121, 122/123

Part of the stage design on page 51 was made by Clive Richardson from components designed by the Deans.

Supplementary Photography
Clive Richardson, 63B, 65B, 67B, 67C
Ian Thompson-Yates, 149I

Acknowledgments

This book is a compilation of several projects and ventures. We would like to express our gratitude to the people whose help and support made things possible:

Donald Lehmkuhl, Karen Hasin-Bromley, Christine Miles, Alexander and Charlotte Mosley, Peter Ledeboer, Steve Henderson, Jean Elford, Cindy Leslie, Kate, Mandy, Bud, Bill and Audry.

RD & MD

ERRATUM

The pages for the chapter openings for Video Pods & Games and Starcodes have been inadvertently switched in this edition.

CONTENTS

ROGER DEAN was born in Kent in 1944. He studied industrial design (furniture) at the Canterbury School of Art from 1961 to 1964, then moved to the Royal College of Art, where he designed the Sea Urchin Chair and an early version of his house. After leaving college in 1968 he designed the seating for "Upstairs" at Ronnie Scott's jazz club. Between 1968 and 1979 he worked on album cover illustrations, designing stage sets between 1972 and 1973, and he still does occasional album graphics. The 1970 Daily Telegraph Design for Living exhibition featured his Teddy Bear Chairs, and in 1975 he had an exhibition of his work at the New York Cultural Center. Also in 1975 Roger Dean formed Dragon's Dream to publish his book Views and in 1976, with Martyn Dean and Hubert Schaafsma, he set up Paper Tiger.

In 1979 he became a director of Magnetic Storm, the design company he formed with Martyn Dean and Robert Fitzgerald to specialise in product research and development, theatrical construction, architectural design, illustrated books, posters and film production. Subsequent projects have included, among others, concept planning and design for theme parks and sports, leisure and marine parks in England, Australia and Finland. Exhibitions of Roger's paintings were held in Los Angeles in 1990 and San Francisco in 1991. He resides with his wife, Amanda, and daughter, Freyja (b. September 16, 1987), on England's South Coast. Roger and Martyn Dean currently are engrossed in the development of the Electronic Personal Orientation Device (E-Pod), a self-contained entertainment center, based on the concept of virtual reality, that surrounds the user and offers the latest in computer game technology.

MARTYN DEAN, also born in Kent (1947), studied industrial design (engineering) from 1965 to 1969 at the Central School of Art and Design. His Retreat Pod and Dinosaur Seating were featured in the 1970 Daily Telegraph Design for Living exhibition. Between 1970 and 1971 he lectured in exhibition design, then he worked as interior designer for the Virgin Record shops. After working on several album cover designs he was a professional photographer in the United States, India and Southeast Asia for seven years. Between 1976 and 1979 he was art director, designer and editor of Dragon's World and Paper Tiger Books, while between 1972 and 1980 he built four rock stage sets, including a giant twenty-foot puppet. He set up and became a director of Magnetic Storm in 1979. Currently he is producing exhibition pieces in the entertainment and computer/video fields, as well as a variety of books. He shares with brother Roger an immersion in the development of E-Pod technology.

PREFACE

Magnetic Storm is a "progress report" by one of the most inventive design teams in Britain: Martyn and Roger Dean. A decade has passed since the brothers published their runaway bestseller *Views*, a decade in which they have extended and developed their already diverse repertoire, from Yes record covers and stages to video games, TV series, publishing and plans for multimillion-pound architectural projects.

During that time their following has continued to grow. A new generation of Dean fans has emerged, for whom the sixties and early seventies rock scene is history. In schools, Roger Dean's paintings have achieved the status of a set topic; in art colleges, he is a pervasive influence and inspiration; and even some critics are now eccentric enough to recognise the value of modern art that dares to be exciting, popular and pleasing to the eye.

In an age of specialists, the diversity of the Deans' talents is out of the ordinary. Roger has, at various times, designed record covers, posters, book jackets, exhibitions, furniture, a toy space station, a children's playground, tree houses, homes, apartments, hotels, office towers, theme parks, the interior of Ronnie Scott's club, lettering for Yes and Asia products, the logo for Virgin Records and a TV advertisement for Sony. Martyn has been a professional photographer of industrial, landscape and rock'n'roll subjects, designed and built stage sets, and designed computer pods, video game consoles and interiors for Virgin Records' shops. They have also lectured and been successful publishers. In 1979 they set up a design company to handle the larger projects in which they were becoming increasingly involved. They called it Magnetic Storm, which gives its name to this book.

Their influence continues to be felt in many of these fields. They share the credit for creating rock merchandising—badges, buckles, programmes, posters, etc.—for groups on tour. (They did it for Yes on their U.S. tour in 1974.) In the art world, they gave credibility to the work of fantasy illustration by commissioning books by the best artists, such as; Syd Mead; Chris Foss, the SF hardware specialist and Frank Hampson, the creator of Dan Dare. This in turn pushed up the going rate for fantasy illustrations by up to five times and created a big demand for such artists. Suddenly, art schools were full of students eager to fill the gap. In the field of typographical design, Roger started a trend by turning words into pictures, re-creating a kind of hieroglyphs. The rock world is still permeated with lookalike Roger Dean lettering.

Views is a hard act to follow. Published in 1975, it sold half a million copies from Tokyo to Tallahassee, Amsterdam to Alice Springs. Nine years, four covers and numerous reprintings later, it is still selling. *Views* was a phenomenon in publishing history. There had never been anything like it. Yet, amazingly, it was Roger and Martyn's first venture in publishing. Their only sales knowledge was of records and posters, so they innocently believed that 100,000 copies was the minimum to aim for. But they knew their market and they had a salable idea.

Views was designed to match the size and shape of a record sleeve—to fit on record shop shelves—and even cost the same as an album. Having decided on the format, the Deans set about producing the most technically perfect picture book possible. They spent fifty times more than a normal publisher would have on a book of that cover price and packed it with several hundred colour plates. Then they released it, with a huge initial print run, on an unsuspecting world. There had been no publicity and no launch, just brilliantly unorthodox entrepreneurial skill. The distributors Big O's target was record and poster stores, not bookshops. As a result, *Views* was a best-seller before the publishing world had even heard of it. At first it was considered a freak, an elaborate hoax; but its success soon proved real enough.

A combination of events made that success possible. First, the market was right. There was an insatiable demand at the time for books about the rock scene. Second, it coincided with an explosion in new, cheap, colour printing technology. This made it possible to combine superb reproduction with low cost. Above all, *Views* had the stamp of the age.

Magnetic Storm continues the story where *Views* left off, looking back frankly at the successes and disappointments of the past ten years, and forward to future ambitions. It traces the work the Deans have done privately and for their company. Most of the paintings, sketches and photographs have never been published before, and many of the projects illustrated, particularly in the architecture and film sections, are still at the planning stage at the time of writing.

Books are the means by which the Deans market their work. They also give life to as-yet-unfinished projects, such as the War of the Worlds paintings and the aircraft livery designs, which would not otherwise be seen. But there is another, deeper purpose. "Everything we do is photographed with a book in mind," Martyn says, "not for portfolios or simply to

make money, but to order things, to collect, catalogue and preserve them for our own use. It is a review, a progress report on our lives."

This approach gives a rare insight into the private world of the artistic imagination. We share the drama of Martyn constructing a stage in the hurly-burly of a rock tour, or Roger piecing together the images of a new painting. Theory and practice are presented side by side: we learn the philosophy behind Roger's radically new "instinctive" architecture and exactly how his space-age homes are built.

Magnetic Storm reflects the Dean brothers' increasing artistic maturity: the new skills they have acquired, often painfully, always meticulously, and the new directions they have taken. The belief that design is an incomplete discipline in itself has driven them to seek other knowledge in different fields. For example, they went into publishing, tackling every aspect from writing and design to commissioning and production, in order to learn about business and management.

It is only fitting, therefore, that this book should finish with the section on architectural design. For this is the end to which they have been directing their energy and assimilating new skills since their art college days. Their artistic impulse has always been to create alternative worlds, more attractive, more exciting, more fantastic, but still our own. They have never peddled fairy tales or pretty notions. They are, at heart, builders. Now, just as a model airplane maker dreams of building the real thing, they are preparing to build the worlds they have dreamt.

David Lucas
September 1984

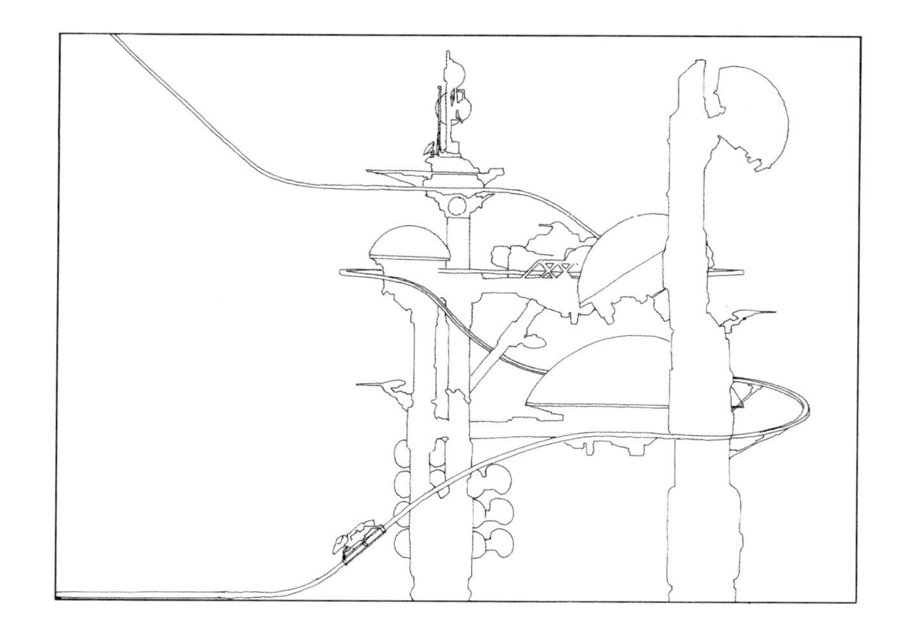

INTRODUCTION

Roger and Martyn's opposite approaches and characters are at the centre of Magnetic Storm's creative force. While Roger takes a meditative approach to each new problem, seeking equilibrium, sketching his way carefully step by step, Martyn likes dynamism, the struggle with circumstance, creative conflict. Roger is a collector, amassing prints, stamps, books on the Crusades, medieval history, science and science fiction and, above all, natural history, as portrayed in both meticulous nineteenth-century illustrations and real life—a hearth full of coral, cacti by the kitchen window. He surrounds his workplace with things he enjoys—categorized information, his own paintings. Martyn, on the other hand, collects nothing. He prefers space to pace up and down in empty rooms with bare floorboards. "Asceticism," Roger calls it, but Martyn disagrees. "There's no virtue in austerity for its own sake. I just hate clutter."

Each lives and works separately, and they cooperate rather than collaborate—criticizing, contributing, exchanging ideas. "Roger controls his world from the end of a pencil. I decide what I want, then seek out the materials and processes that will get me there. We think completely differently, but from opposite directions we often arrive at similar conclusions."

Many of the design projects illustrated in this book have complex histories reaching back to the earliest days of Roger and Martyn's professional careers. They have been picked up, put down, rethought, turned around, stopped and started again, in multiple negotiations with changing partners; and some still have not yielded their final product. As Roger says, "Of the thousands of letters and sketches I have, which ones actually carried the story forward? Sorting through all our efforts is frequently awful, occasionally fascinating and sometimes quite encouraging."

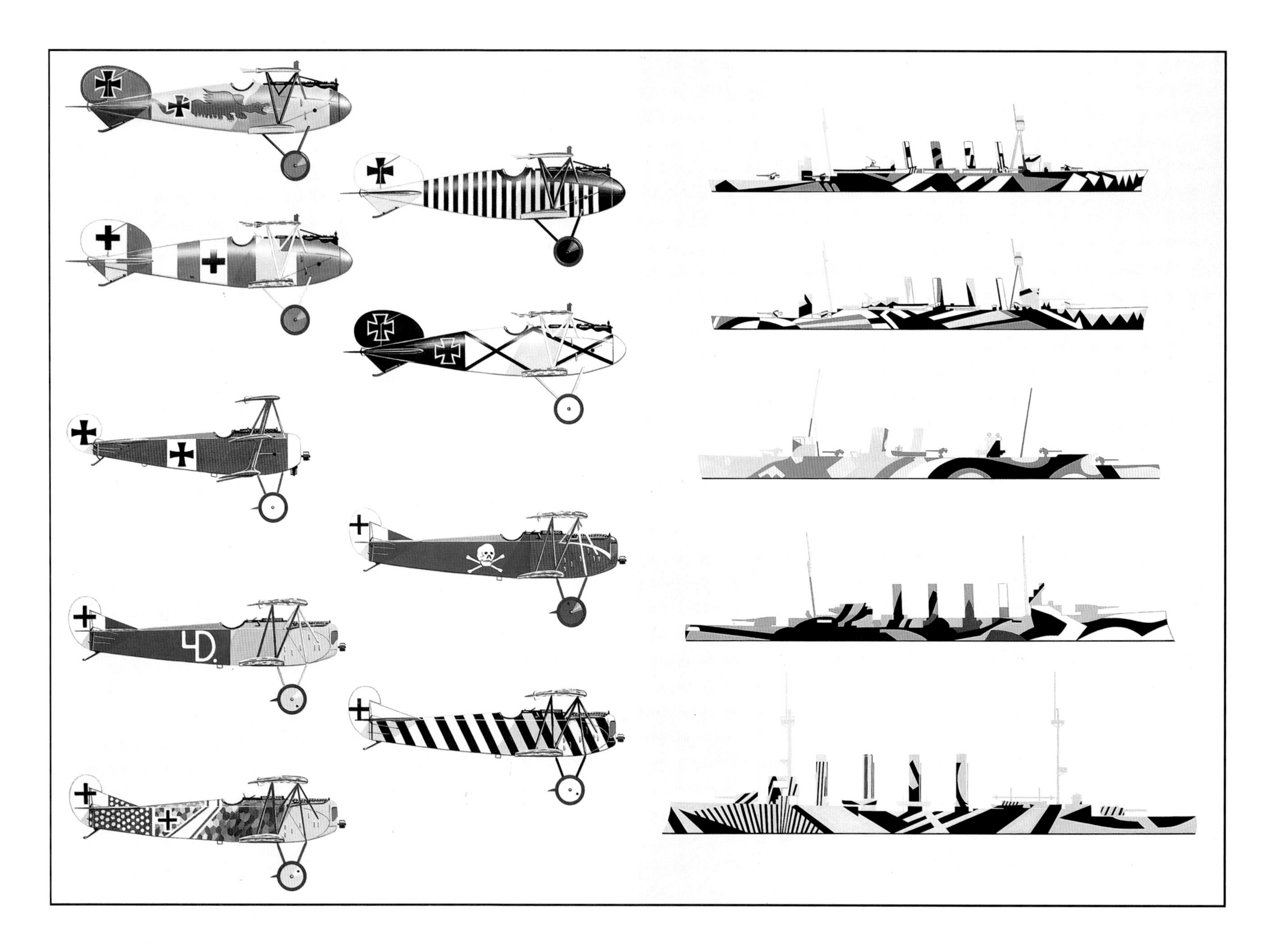

When the Deans were students it was the convention that decoration was mere embellishment and as such was not worth considering in terms of "serious" industrial design. This attitude was a leftover from the heady austerity of Functionalism, Bauhaus and its joyless ilk, whose precepts decreed that surfaces be plain and unadorned, that form follow function, and that the finished object's appearance be determined by the physical structure of its material. In the natural world, however, whose forms are such a powerful influence on the Deans' architectural and design ideas, surface markings are of vital importance, either as camouflage or as display. Irregular speckles or stripes blend with the undergrowth, the peacock's plumage is an advertisement for a mate, the wasp's black and yellow stripes are a warning.

"Markings in themselves are fascinating," says Roger, "and often astonishingly beautiful. It seemed to me that the markings on the tiger or the tabby cat were part of the essence of the creature, and not there without a purpose; and if they had a purpose there, the principle might be applicable elsewhere. I became interested in the role of surface markings as they might be applied to the man-made object, the product of the designer. At one stage, when we were involved in publishing, we started commissioning pictures for a big book on camouflage and patterns—everything from the Phantom Jet to the Tiger Tank."

The book was to be a celebration of patterning in all its guises, and a demonstration that an object's purpose may be defined not only by its form but also by its surface. Military

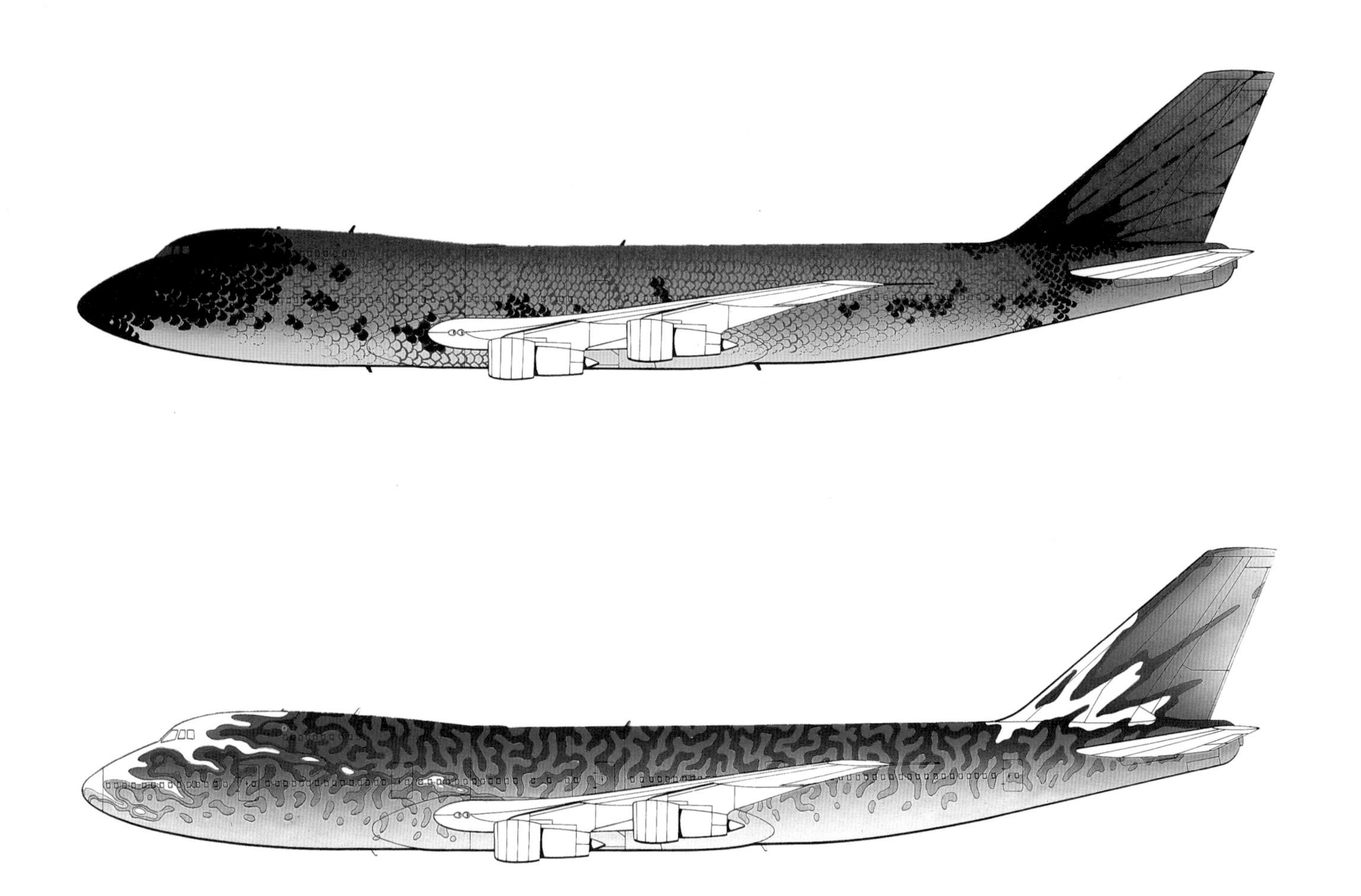

equipment is a good example of this. It is not just an aeroplane's guns that make it look like a weapon, but also the markings it displays—camouflage to conceal it from above and below, and insignia to show to which side it belongs. Planes decorated with brightly coloured dragons, however martial they may appear, are clearly not warplanes. Magnetic Storm's aircraft designs (see above) were proposals for a holiday airline that approached them for a new livery.

As well as the influence of natural forms and patterns, emphasis on multimedia presentation and interlocking projects is characteristic of Roger and Martyn's work. This is something they regard as almost a matter of course, having always found concentrating on a single aspect of a design limiting. As their company name implies, nothing is fixed. An album cover will incorporate an architectural suggestion, graphics for a music video will give rise to T-shirts and badges, a two-dimensional idea might work equally successfully in three, or vice versa, though often with vastly different results. Each design solution can be taken as a piece of the Dean "worldview" if you like, one small section of a cumulative whole. If your chair is uncomfortable and awkward, design a new one. Then you will need a new room for your new chair, a new house for your new room, a new city for your new house, a new landscape for your new city. A new kind of tree house needs a new kind of tree. A new object needs a new environment, a new universe.

One example of this total design approach is the Sydney Harbour project (see p. 163), and another, albeit less spectacular, is their precision model space station for children and adults (see p. 11). Conceived in the early seventies, this was to be a scientifically accurate and highly detailed scale construction sold in kit form that could be assembled at home and would include such realistic features as plug-in accommodations and work modules. An accompanying video game would enable the player to participate in all aspects of running the space station. The project attracted the attention of a leading toy company, which later had to withdraw due to financial difficulties on another front. The project, however, continues in search of a backer and, like so much else of the Deans' work, in a constant state of evolution.

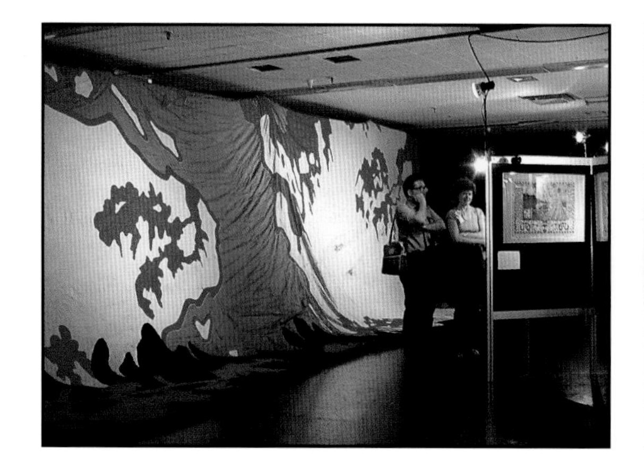

Another project that focused the wide range of Magnetic Storm's interests and output was their involvement in the World Science Fiction Convention held at Brighton in 1979. The Deans have had a long association with science fiction and fantasy, its publication, packaging and accompanying merchandise, and have visited several other conventions. This Worldcon (Seacon for the occasion) seemed an excellent opportunity to show their work, talk to visiting writers and artists, and meet the fans and the public at large. Christine Miles, Roger's personal assistant at the time, and secretarial assistant Shelley Alge organised and coordinated the company's Seacon exhibition, filling an entire hall with their architecture, books, posters and artwork. The specially bought display system was augmented with backdrops and sections from their stage sets.

Since its inception, the structure of Magnetic Storm has altered to suit the project in hand, taking on personnel and workplaces as necessary. Roger's first publications were edited, designed and laid out in his own home. Christine Miles started her career with the company by organizing an exhibition of Roger's work and taking it to New York, all before her eighteenth birthday. Shelley Alge joined as secretarial assistant; Donald Lehmkuhl as senior editor and advisor for Dragon's Dream, then for Paper Tiger; and Jim Slattery was taken on as text editor and art historian. As the numbers increased Magnetic Storm took over an old Brighton school and refitted it as company offices.

When, at the end of the seventies, the company expanded into construction projects such as the Taitan heads (see p. 42) and the Crystal stage (see p. 54), their offices' interior was converted into workshops and showplace areas, with emphasis on the firm's capabilities in three-dimensional design and manufacture.

Now things have come full circle, with Martyn and Roger working once again from their own studios. Even so, the scope of Magnetic Storm's activities, having ranged from record covers to film and television projects, rock stage sets to publishing, architecture and landscaping to Space Invaders machines, Victorian fantasy to video games, is wider than ever. "Essentially," Roger remarks, "I see no difference between designing a logo and designing a hotel. The criteria you use are radically different, but the thought processes are surprisingly similar: the drive for aesthetic satisfaction through an elegant solution to the problem."

Here, then, are just a few of their solutions.

Coral island

Coral island

Pace

Pace

PUBLISHING

PUBLISHING

The ambitious character of Roger's publishing enterprises conceals the fact that originally he never intended to enter the business at all, and did so with some trepidation. He always hoped to compile a book of his work; indeed, some of his designs were never intended to go beyond the printed page. Many others were practical solutions to design problems and would be built, lived with and used. The Sea Urchin Chair was a universal design that could be sat in from any direction. Another seating idea was the suggestion that one should grow a comfortable tail, and thus be able to sit wherever one wished. When Roger designed an original kind of tree house, he also designed the tree in which to build it. Without the help of an indulgent deity, the only public life for these notions was as pictures in a book.

In 1968, immediately after graduating from the Royal College of Art, Roger Dean went to the art publishers Studio Vista with a proposal for a book of archetypal architecture, based on his college thesis. They were interested and discussions continued for six months before a new editor arrived and put paid to the idea. As Roger's professional career blossomed and his portfolio filled, he kept knocking on editors' doors, eighteen in all, around London and New York. His friend Alexander Mosley was keen on the book and tried to help Roger place it with his employers, Mitchell Beazley, but they had no more luck there than anywhere else.

With one hundred and sixty pages of full-colour and fine-tone reproductions, Roger's collection was certainly going to be expensive to produce; but the more copies printed, the less each one would cost. Peter Ledeboer of Big O had already guaranteed to take ninety thousand for distribution, hoping to build on the success they were having with his posters. With that kind of print run, the book could be retailed for no more than the price of a long-playing record, as Roger had always intended, but no publisher had been convinced.

Peter introduced Roger to Hubert Schaafsma, U.K. sales representative of the Dutch printers Chevalier, who were eager for work like this. Alexander Mosley was now working in Paris for KIM. This company originally agreed to publish *Views* but pulled out at the last moment. It seemed the only way *Views* would ever see print was for Roger to publish it himself. He had all the material in page proofs already, though he'd had to mortgage everything he owned to pay for them. He had a printer, a distributor and a ton of sympathetic advice. But was he prepared to become a publisher?

Roger Dean
Views

Roger Dean
Views

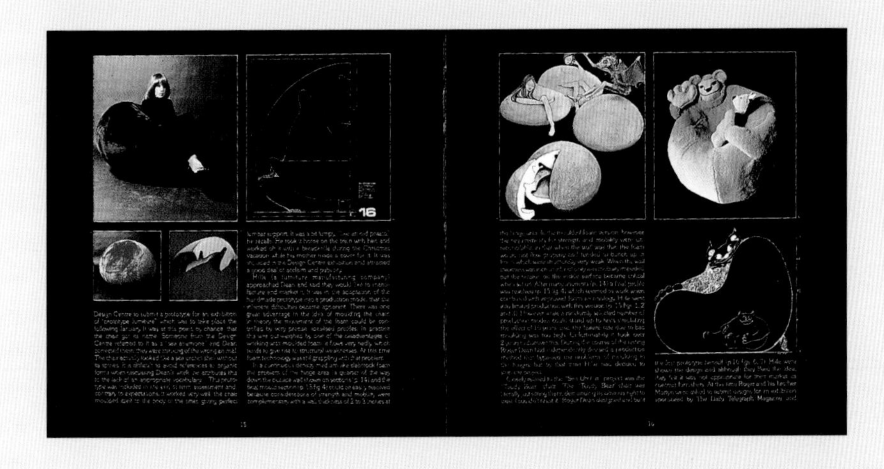

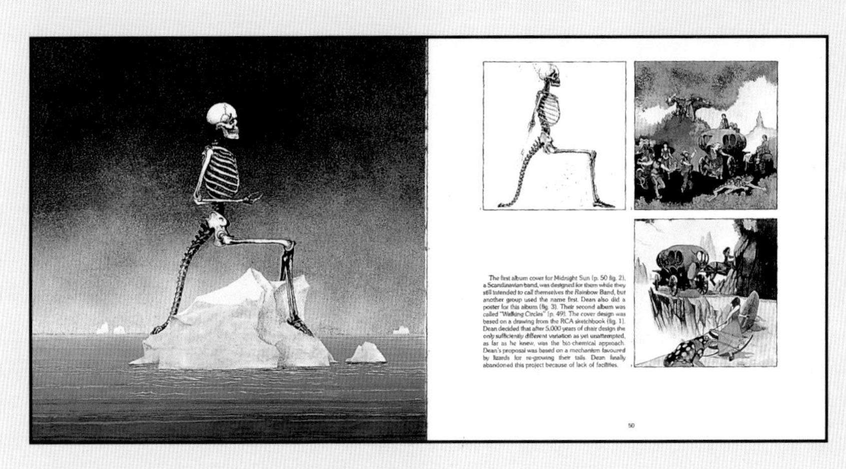

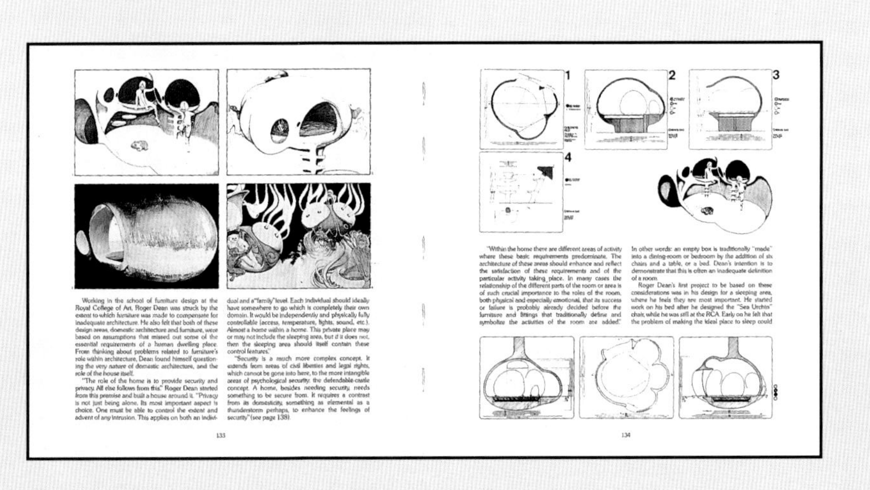

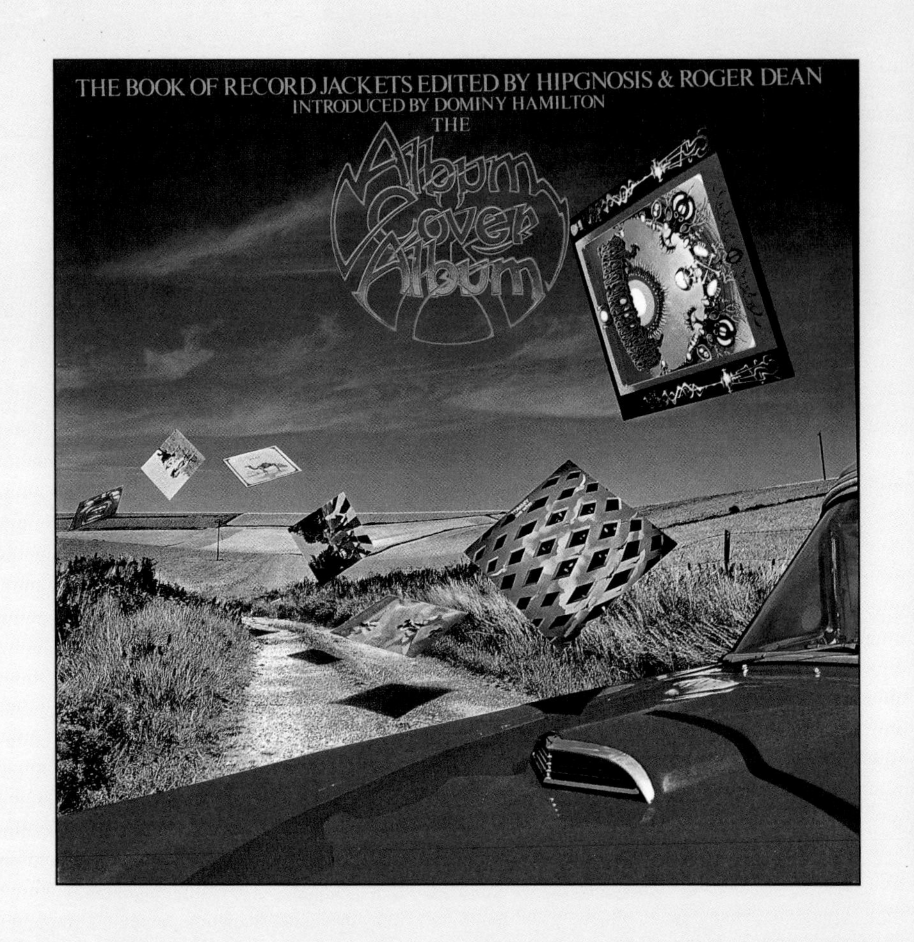
THE BOOK OF RECORD JACKETS EDITED BY HIPGNOSIS & ROGER DEAN
INTRODUCED BY DOMINY HAMILTON
THE
Album Cover Album

THE 2ND BOOK OF RECORD SLEEVES COMPILED BY ROGER DEAN AND DAVID HOWELLS
The Second Volume
Album Cover Album

FREDDIE HUBBARD
LIQUID LOVE

U.K. SUBS

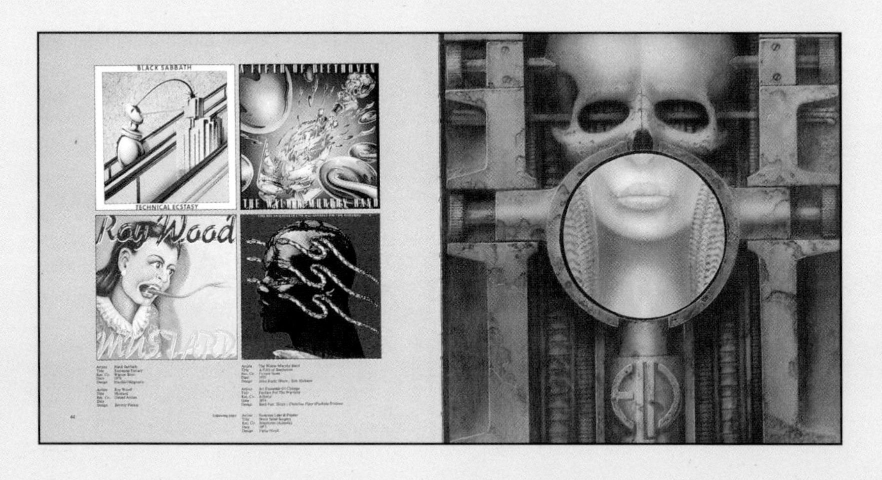
BLACK SABBATH
TECHNICAL ECSTASY
Roy Wood

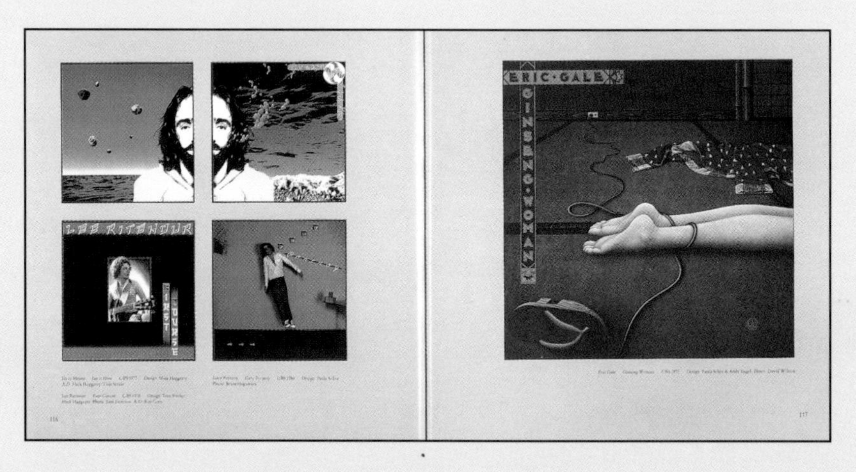
ERIC GALE
GINSENG WOMAN

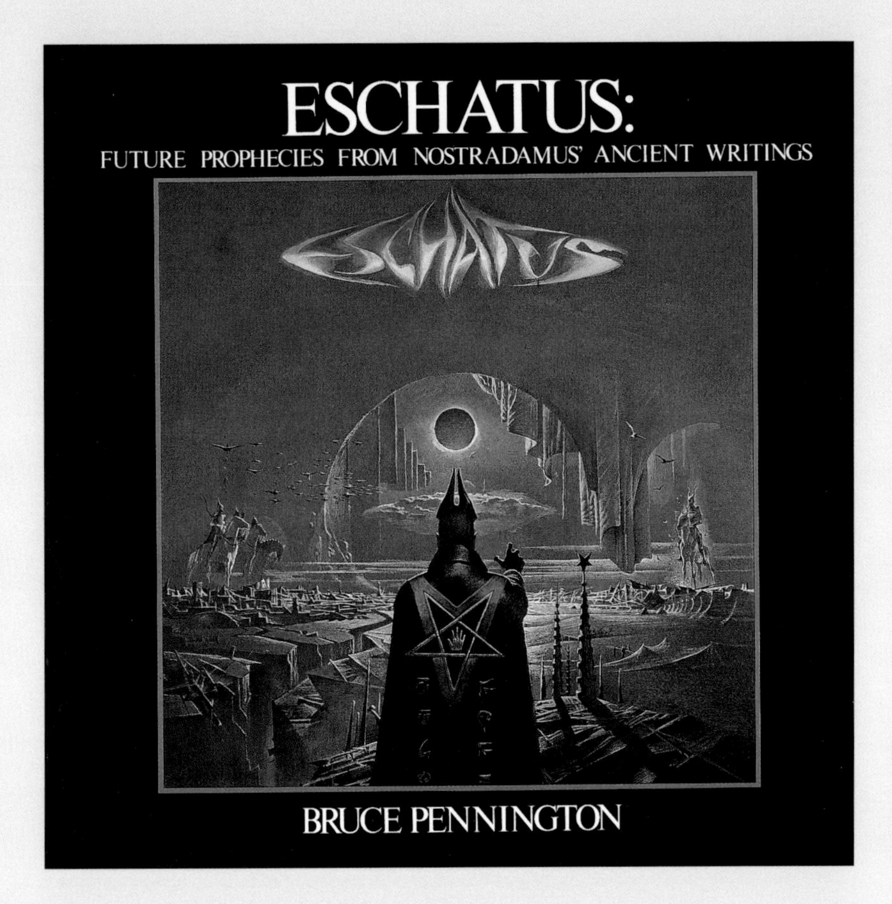
ESCHATUS:
FUTURE PROPHECIES FROM NOSTRADAMUS' ANCIENT WRITINGS
BRUCE PENNINGTON

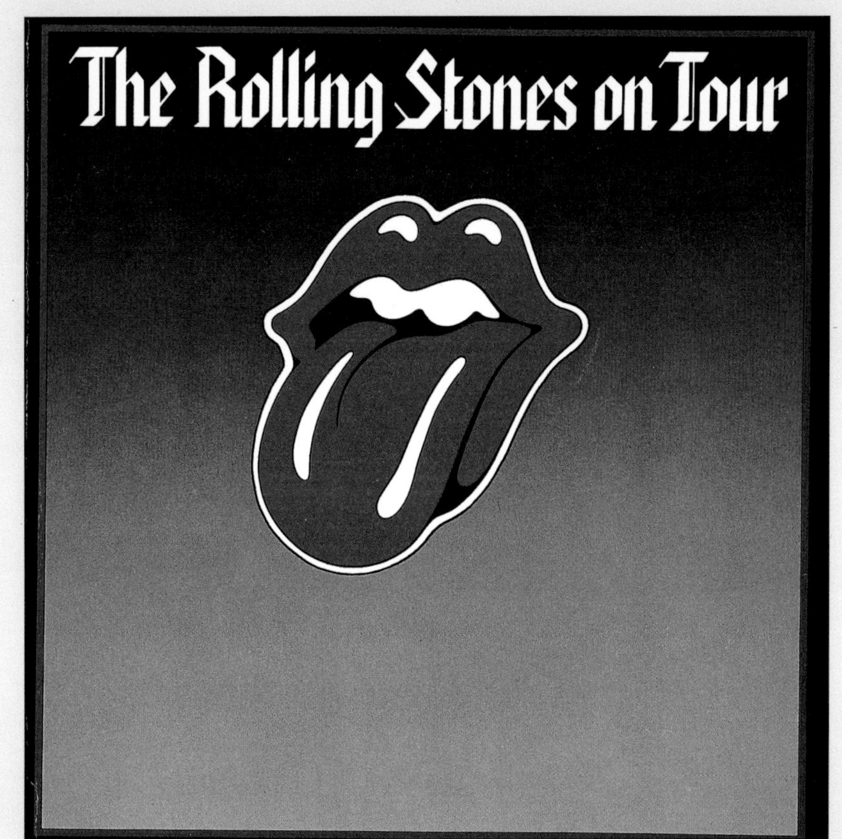
The Rolling Stones on Tour

The Flights of
Icarus

The Pentateuch

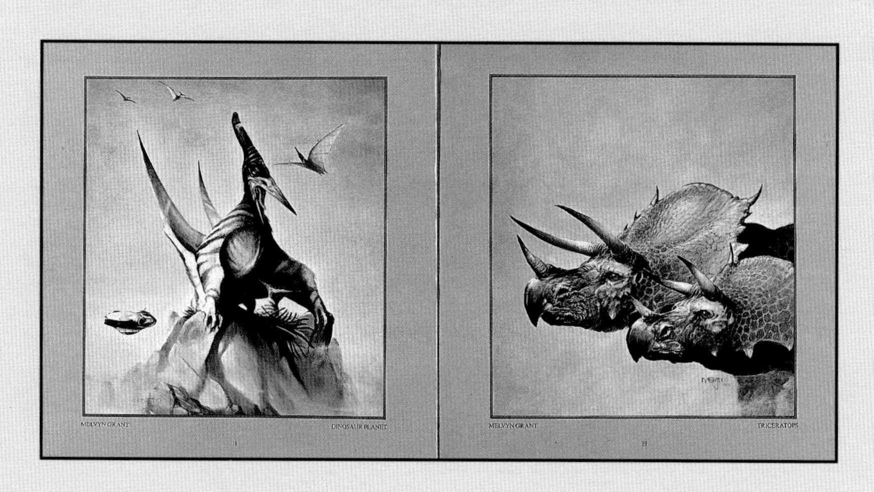
MELVYN GRANT
DINOSAUR PLANET
MELVYN GRANT
TRICERATOPS

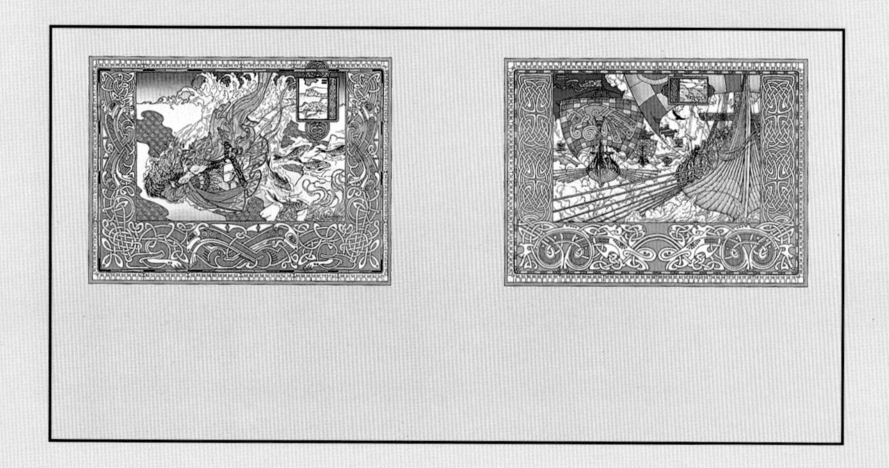

THE STUDIO

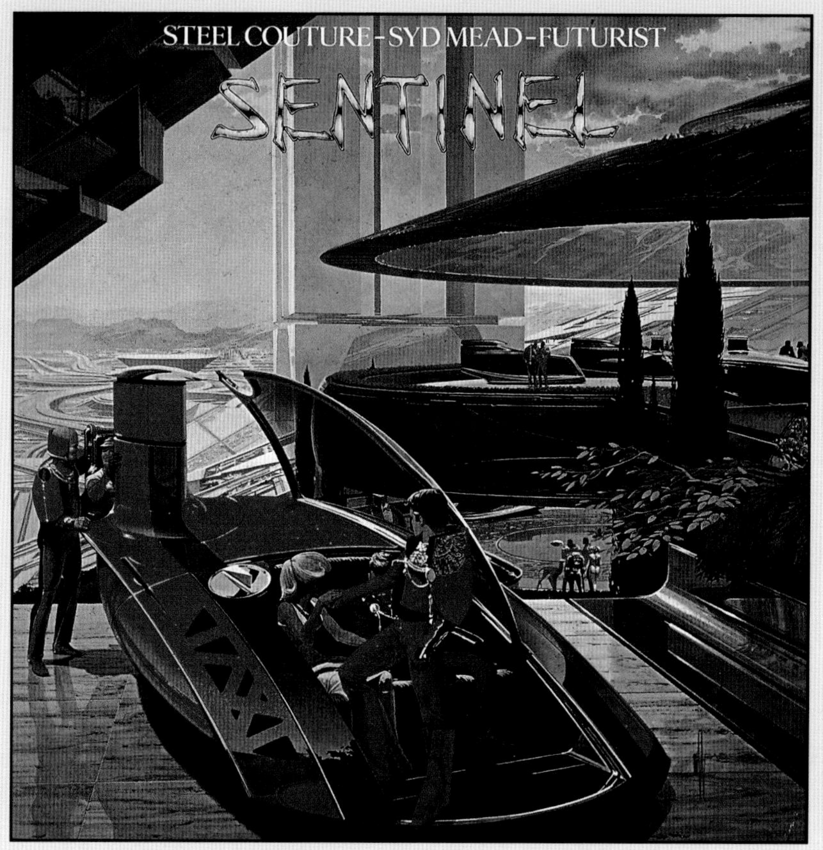
STEEL COUTURE - SYD MEAD - FUTURIST
SENTINEL

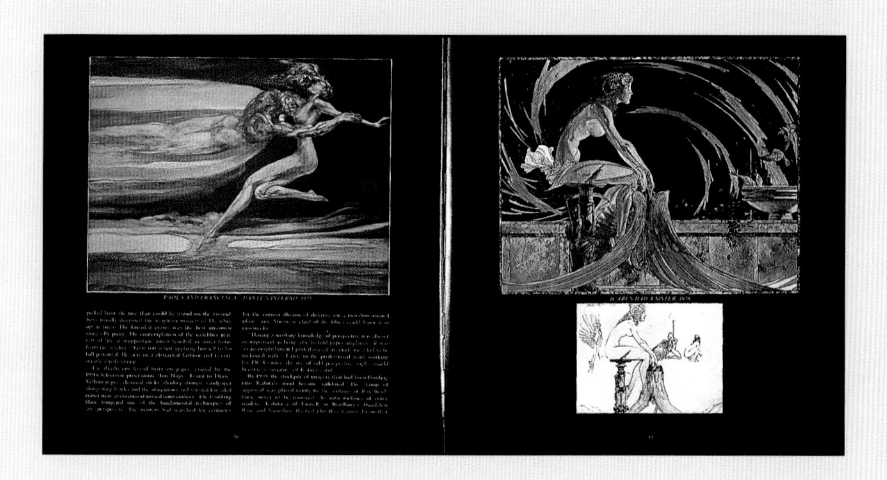

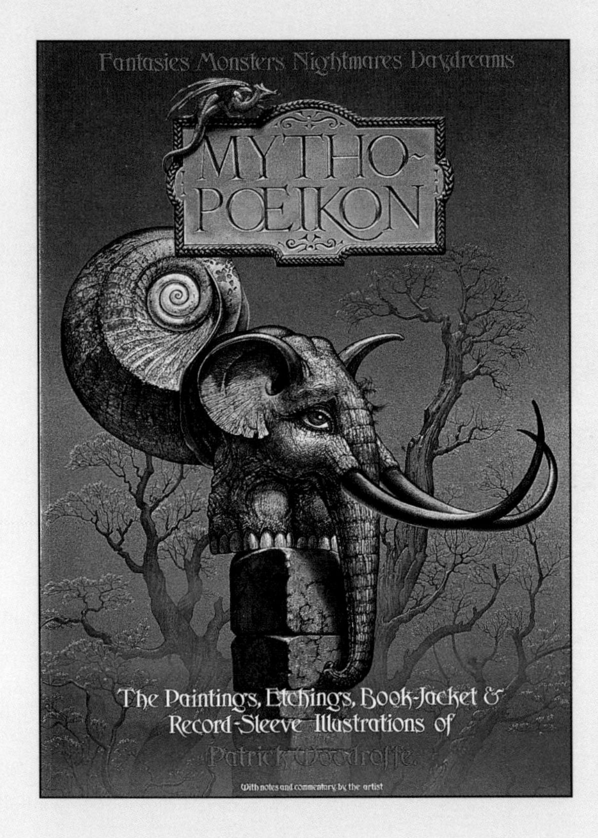

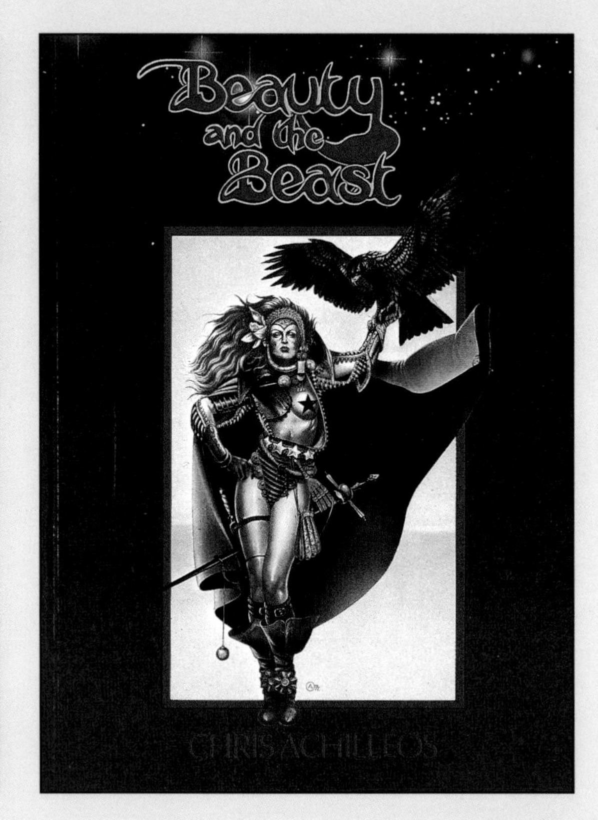

Roger consulted the *I Ching*, the ancient Chinese oracle. The hexagram he cast was *Ch'ien*: "Creativity. Supreme success. Perseverance in the right way brings good fortune." *Ch'ien* is the most positive answer the *I Ching* can give. Traditionally its six unbroken lines are known as dragons; and as 1975 was the Year of the Dragon, the new publishing company became Dragon's Dream.

Working round the clock from Roger's home in Brighton, the new team battled against disasters and deadlines to make the dream a reality. Nobody involved had any experience of book publication. "None of us knew that we didn't know what we were doing," says Roger, "but we knew exactly what we wanted."

First sales of *Views*, at Christmas through poster and record shops, confirmed the unqualified optimism of the *I Ching*, not to mention the investment of Big O. Even before the book trade had ever heard of *Views*, Roger saw the spectre of bankruptcy begin to fade away. When Big O moved into bookshop distribution some weeks later, the seasonal rush was over, but sales were still high enough to put *Views* straight in at number one on the *Sunday Times* best-seller list. The trade journal *The Bookseller* asked frostily: "Is this a practical joke?" It was not. It was a new kind of publishing.

Views stayed at number one for nearly a month and went on to sell half a million copies. Chevalier had agreed to follow it with a string of Roger's other projects but apparently were not as committed to them as he was, despite the instant success of *Views*. In 1976, Roger and Hubert Schaafsma set up a second company to publish books under an imprint with the whimsical and evocative name of Paper Tiger. Unfortunately, the company itself was registered as Dragon's World Ltd., later to be a source of some confusion, as Dragon's Dream also continued to publish books.

The first Paper Tiger book was to be a history of record covers—an obvious winner that somebody was bound to do sooner or later. In fact, when Roger asked his old college friend Storm Thorgerson to contribute some of his studio's designs, Storm told him he was already working on the same idea. They combined forces and, with extra research by David

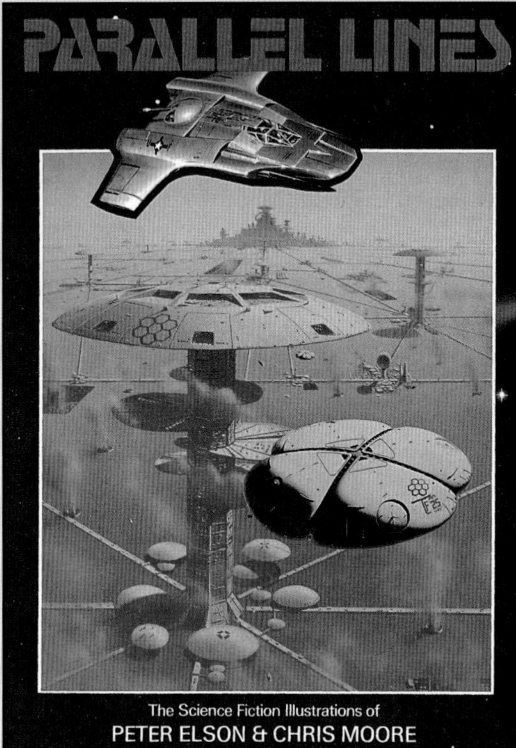

Howells and a historical survey by Dominy Hamilton, completed *The Album Cover Album*. The selection and editing, Roger recalls, were a pleasure, not least because it involved meeting artists he had admired and collected for years, sometimes buying records just for the sleeves: Rick Griffin, Kelley and Mouse, and Michael English.

Roger and Martyn were later to produce individual books by all these artists, while Storm's work with Aubrey Powell as Hipgnosis was collected in *Walk Away René* in 1980.

When *The Album Cover Album* came out in 1977, rock music was in upheaval, and sleeve design changed radically. Gone were the lavish and exuberant sleeves of psychedelia and progressive rock; in came severity and austere graphics borrowed from the thirties and the fifties. It was already time to begin the second volume, collecting punk and new wave albums, along with a wider look at jazz and classical design and sample sleeves from Japan, which many Western fans would not have seen otherwise. Volume three will follow soon, bringing the story up to date.

One band that had not been washed away by the new wave was The Rolling Stones. They were about to leave for America and wanted a compilation of photographs by Annie Leibowitz and Christopher Sykes, taken on an earlier visit, out in time for the tour. The problem was that there was ten times too much material and only four weeks in which to produce the book. Dragon's Dream promised to have it edited, printed, published and distributed across the States before opening night. They kept the promise. Roger finished the editing in two days flat. "We didn't cut corners; we framed the pictures, put in tinted borders, made it exactly the way we wanted it. Sometimes having to do things in a rush can be very effective."

For Roger Dean, music, words and pictures belong together. It was only a matter of time before he produced the first combined illustrated book and record album. He planned a collaboration between Ramases, who founded 10cc, and Bruce Pennington, whose distinctive book covers have made the alien landscapes of science fiction his own. As far as Roger knew, Bruce had been working for months on illustrating the Book of Revelations for Paper Tiger; but when, after a year, Roger asked how it was going, Bruce announced that

THE WORK OF
HIPGNOSIS
'WALK AWAY RENÉ'

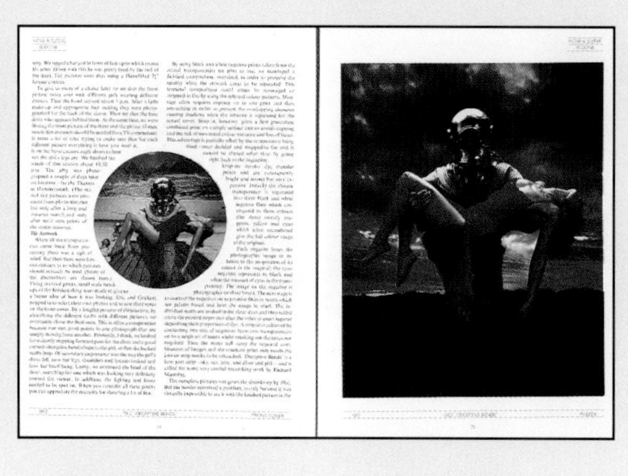

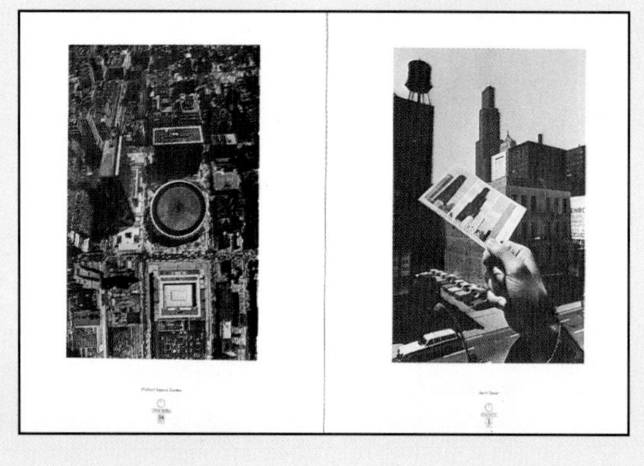

"HANDS ACROSS THE WATER"
WINGS TOUR USA
PHOTOGRAPHS BY HIPGNOSIS

THE EXPEDITION JOURNAL OF PLINY THE ELDER
INVENTORUM
NATURA
UnaWoodruff

Dragonfly Plant
Butterfly Plant

AMARANT
THE FLORA AND FAUNA OF ATLANTIS
BY A LADY BOTANIST
UNA WOODRUFF

FROM SPRING EQUINOX 1978 TO SPRING EQUINOX 1979
1978
1979
THE PHENOMENON BOOK OF CALENDARS
CHINESE
GREGORIAN WESTERN CIVILIAN
HINDU HEBREW ISLAMIC
AZTEC MAYAN I CHING
ZODIACAL RURAL MIGRATION
FAIRS CARNIVALS FESTIVAL DAYS
Yearly Calendar Poster Included

The Round Art
The Astrology of Time and Space
A.T. Mann

THE PHENOMENON BOOK OF CALENDARS 1979·1980
by
Giuseppe Maria Sesti–A.T. Mann IV
Mary Flanagan–Painton Cowen
CHINESE
GREGORIAN WESTERN CIVILIAN
HINDU–HEBREW ISLAMIC
AZTEC MAYAN I CHING
ZODIACAL RURAL MIGRATION
ROMAN NEW GUINEA BALI
FAIRS CARNIVALS FESTIVAL DAYS
Yearly Calendar Poster Included

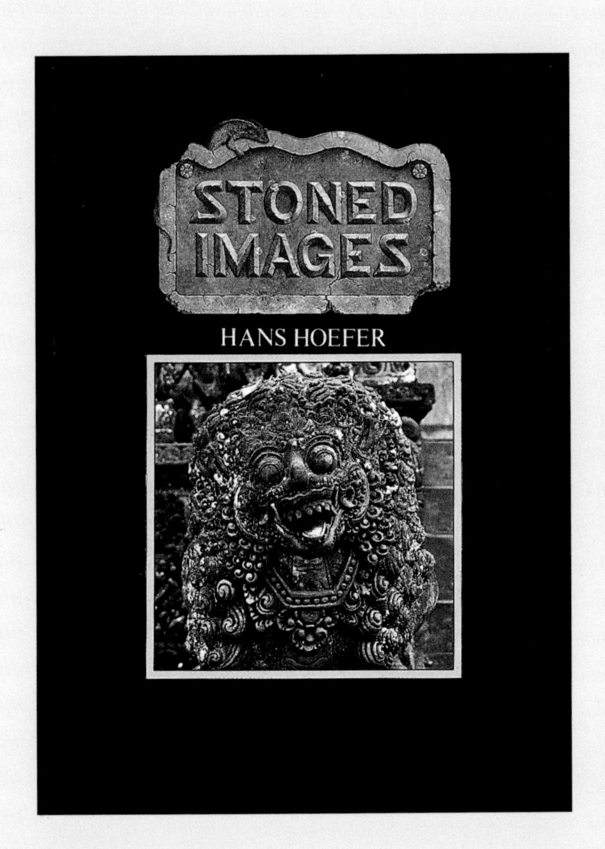
STONED IMAGES
HANS HOEFER

THE ASSOCIATION OF ILLUSTRATORS
THIRD ANNUAL

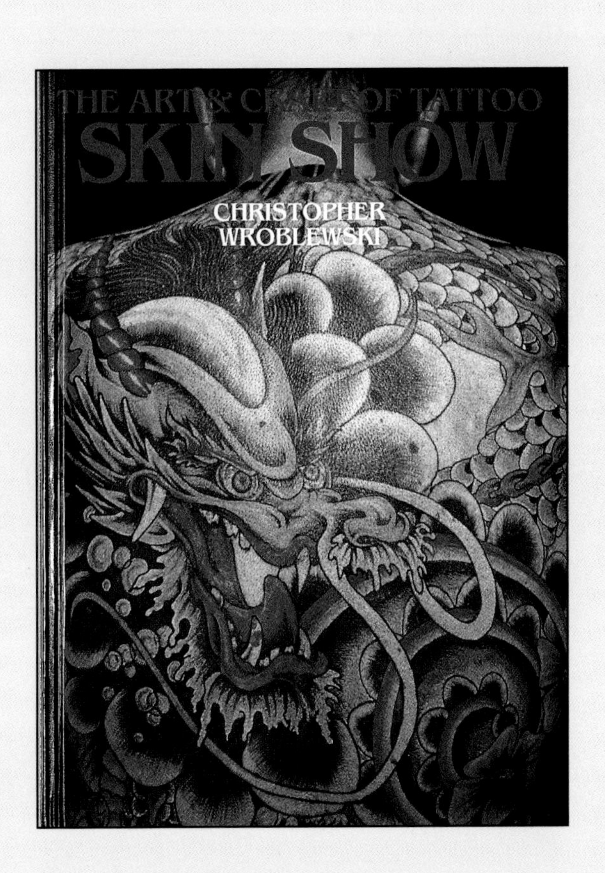
SKIN SHOW
CHRISTOPHER WROBLEWSKI

THE SILVER ARM

lebor gabala érenn

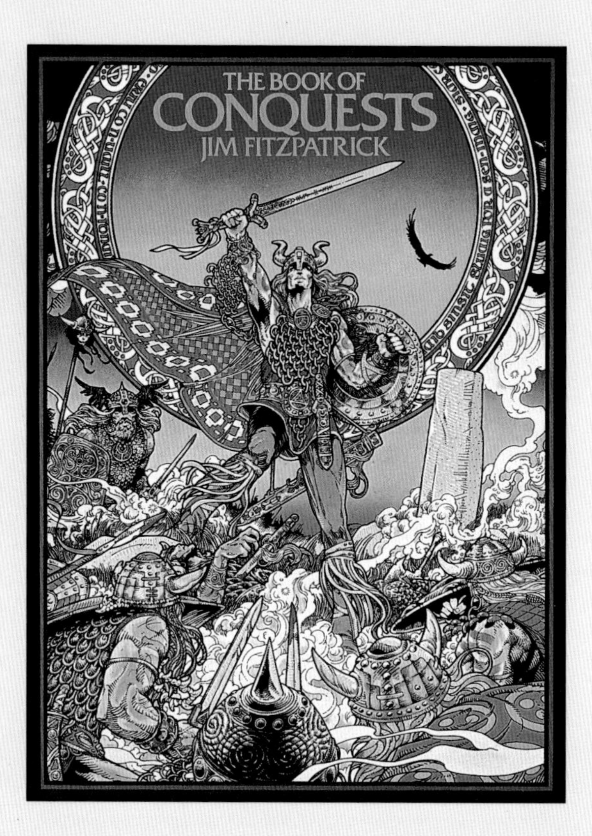
THE BOOK OF CONQUESTS
JIM FITZPATRICK

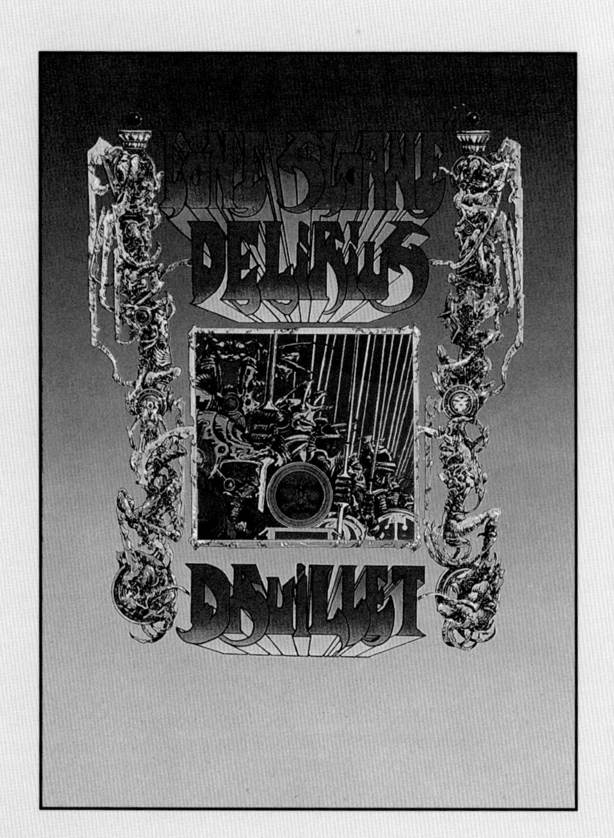
DELIRIUS
DRUILLET

YRAGAEL URM
DRUILLET

DAN DARE
PILOT OF THE FUTURE
IN
THE MAN FROM NOWHERE
VOLUME ONE

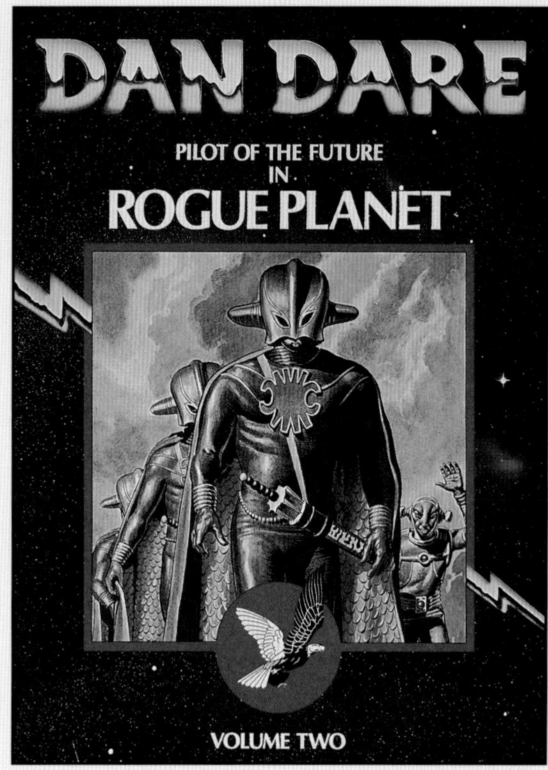
DAN DARE
PILOT OF THE FUTURE
IN
ROGUE PLANET
VOLUME TWO

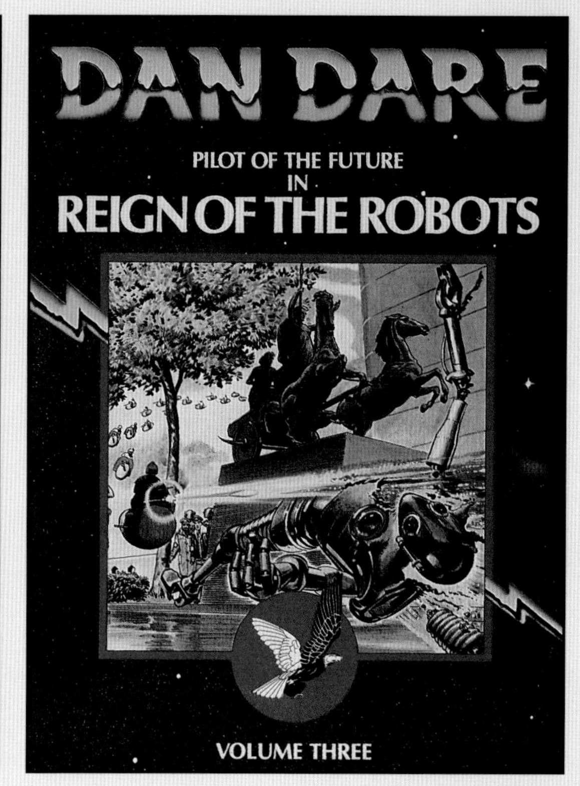
DAN DARE
PILOT OF THE FUTURE
IN
REIGN OF THE ROBOTS
VOLUME THREE

THE
ROAD OF COURAGE
THE STORY OF
JESUS OF NAZARETH
ILLUSTRATED BY FRANK HAMPSON
WRITTEN BY MARCUS MORRIS

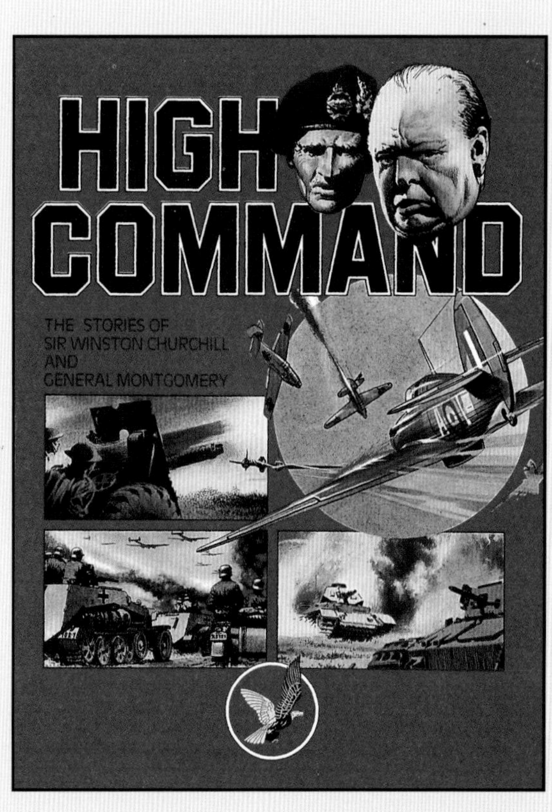
HIGH
COMMAND
THE STORIES OF
SIR WINSTON CHURCHILL
AND
GENERAL MONTGOMERY

Green Dog Trumpet
and other stories
Ian Miller

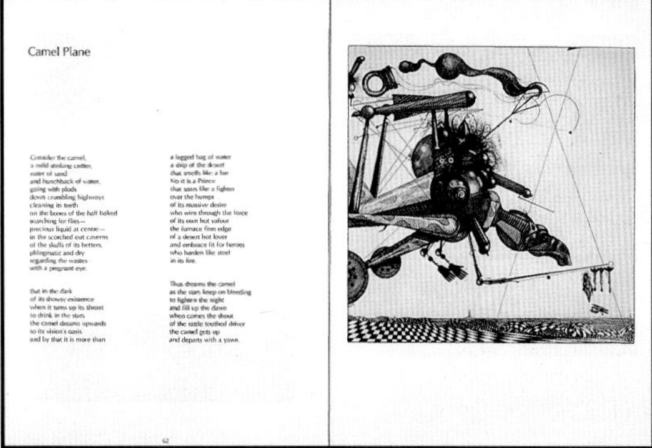
Camel Plane

Secret
Art
Ian Miller

JEFF JONES
IDYL

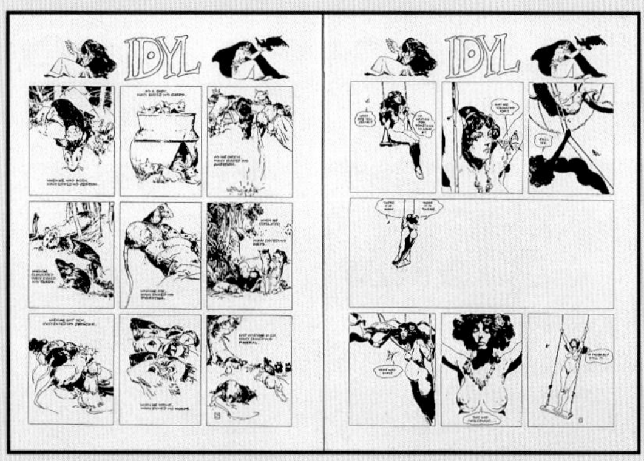
IDYL
IDYL

PHILIP CASTLE

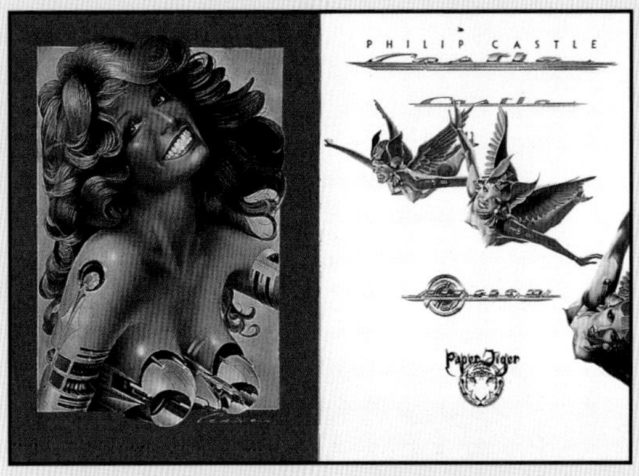
PHILIP CASTLE

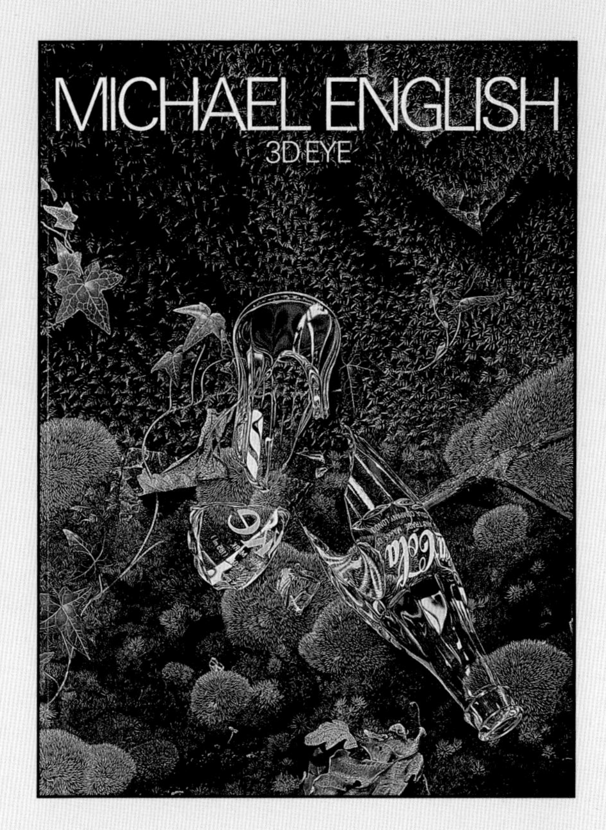
MICHAEL ENGLISH
3D EYE

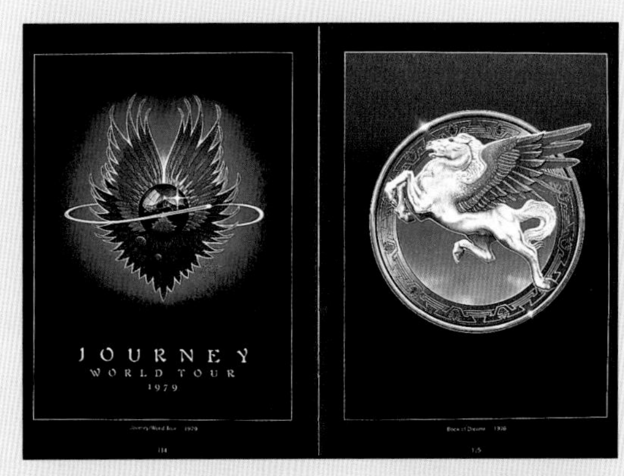
JOURNEY
WORLD TOUR
1979

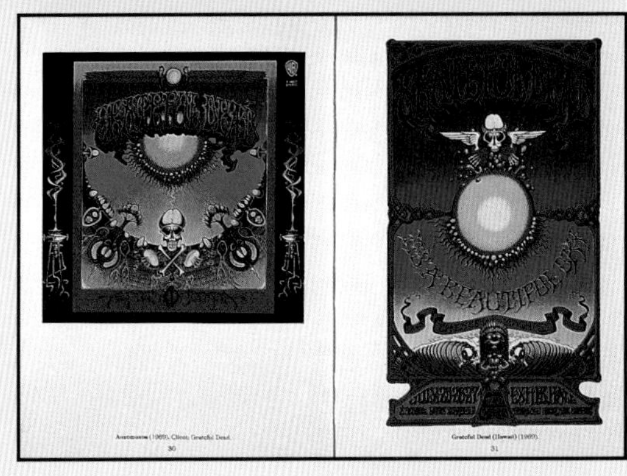

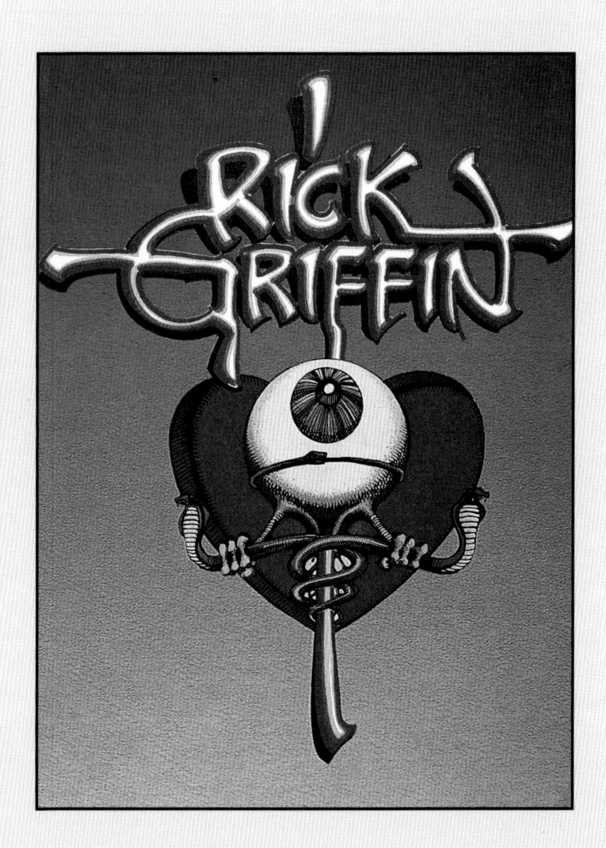
RICK
GRIFFIN

there was a curse on anyone meddling with the Book of Revelations, so he had switched to the prophecies of Nostradamus instead. The result was *Eschatus*, published in 1978.

The book-album Paper Tiger eventually published, with EMI, was *The Pentateuch*, by Patrick Woodroffe and Dave Greenslade. Patrick had painted the sleeve for the Greenslade album *Time and Tide*. It seemed logical to bring them together again, especially since Paper Tiger had already published two Woodroffe books, his retrospective *Mythopoeikon* and his children's story *The Adventures of Tinker the Hole-Eating Duck*. His idea for *The Pentateuch* was a translation of the first five books of an alien Bible discovered in an abandoned spacecraft. Dave Greenslade provided the music.

When an American publisher asked Paper Tiger to compile an anthology of science fiction and fantasy art, Roger and Martyn were already preparing books by Alan Lee, Ian Miller, Jeffrey Jones, Chris Foss and many others. The material was as diverse as it was copious: dinosaurs and dragonflies, flying carpets and spaceships, Egyptian mystery and Celtic filigree. The problem was how to present it all under one unifying title: Donald Lehmkuhl suggested *The Works of Daedalus*. Martyn wryly observed that since few of the mechanical titans looked capable of flight, his son Icarus would provide a more suitable name. Donald composed a mythical history of the universe encapsulated in the seven moments of creation that flash before Icarus's eyes as he tumbles into the sea: the dinosaurs began, and the spaceships concluded *The Flights of Icarus*.

Since several artists the Deans wanted to work with lived in America, Martyn and Al Mosley visited in 1977 and '78. Four of the artists they were looking for were Jeffrey Jones, Michael Kaluta, Barry Windsor-Smith and Berni Wrightson. They found them all in one room sharing the Studio, a twelfth-story loft in lower Manhattan, which they ran like a fin de siècle salon. "The tension of activity in there was electric," Martyn recalls: "It was an almost magical environment." Out of it came a rich and bizarre collection, *The Studio*, in 1979 and Jeffrey Jones's *Idyl* and *Yesterday's Lily* the following year.

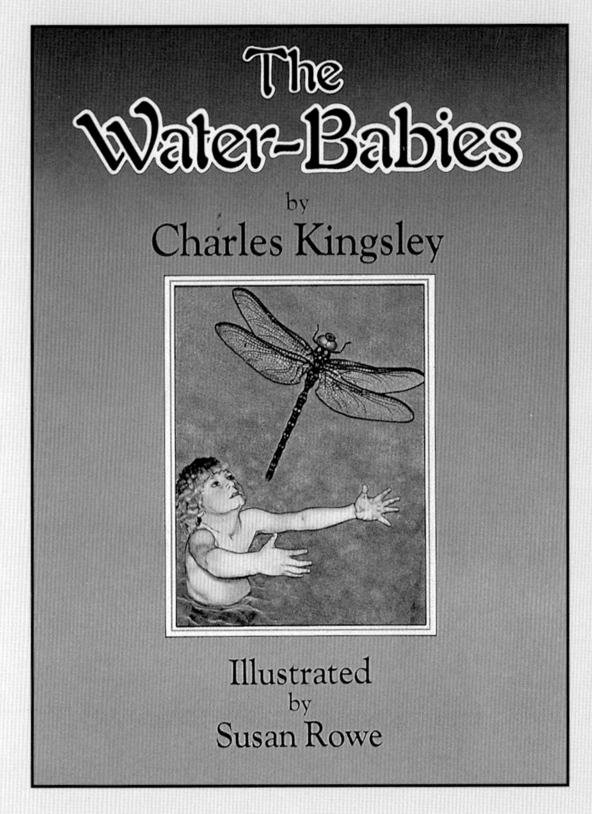

The next stop on the U.S. tour was to be Detroit, to pick up early works by Syd Mead. But this was the grim winter of 1978 and Detroit was snowed up solid. The only flight out of New York that afternoon was to California, and it was leaving right away. There was not even time to telephone England. California did not sound such a bad option. Martyn brought his schedule forward two weeks and headed west. In no time at all he was talking to Syd in the sun and the only ice to be seen was in the cocktails. Syd, whose work Dragon's Dream published in *Sentinel*, is an industrial futurist: everything he paints could be built. "Science fiction artists fantasize about the future," Roger explains. "Syd Mead designs it."

Crossing the bridge from San Francisco and heading north to Marin County you see the two sides of the American Dream. The place still has something of the casual life-style of the sixties, affectionately encapsulated in the designs of Stanley Mouse and Alton Kelley. Whereas Syd Mead's high-tech paradise is sophisticated, rational, cool, their visionary city is spontaneous, sensual, funky. Between the two stretches is Highway One, up which Martyn drove in a nine-seater limou- sine—the only car the hire company had left—to collect the pictures for *Mouse & Kelley*, the Paper Tiger book of their "street heraldry."

Meanwhile, on the other side of the Atlantic, Roger was planning to reprint some illustrated work that was thoroughly British. As boys, both he and Martyn had been keen on *Eagle*, the best of British comics. There was enough material for twenty books, especially in Frank Hampson's strip *Dan Dare—Pilot of the Future*; but when they came to search for the original artwork in the basement archives of IPC, virtually all of it had disappeared. They had to photograph old bound copies of the comic, severely yellowed. Reproduction on clean white paper would only have emphasized the murky quality of the colour, so it was decided to clean up the illustrations as much as possible and use black borders.

Dragon's Dream also published Frank Hampson's biblical story *Road of Courage*, which Roger and Martyn affectionately refer to as "Dan Dare as Christ." In the same heroic vein were Frank Bellamy's pictorial biographies of Winston Churchill and Field Marshal Montgomery, reissued in one volume as *High Command*.

horses and their arms, and thou thyself her prisoner.' That was had forthwith.

And the third day Peredur came to the meadow, and he overthrew more that day than any day else. And at last the earl came to encounter him, and he threw him to the ground, and the earl asked for quarter. 'Who art thou then?' asked Peredur. 'I will not conceal myself,' said he, 'I am the earl.' 'Aye,' said he, 'the whole of her earldom to the maiden, and further, thine own earldom too, and meat for three hundred men, and their drink, and their horses and their arms, and thou thyself in her power.'

And Peredur was thus enforcing tribute and submission to the maiden three weeks. And after establishing and settling her into her dominion, 'With thy leave,' said Peredur, 'I will set out on my way.' 'Is that, my brother, what thou desirest?' 'Aye, by my faith, and had it not been for love of thee I had not been here long

170

since.' 'Friend,' said she, 'who art thou then?' 'Peredur son of Efrawg, out of the North. And if either affliction or peril come upon thee, send to let me know, and I will defend thee if I can.'

Then Peredur set out, and far from thence there met him a lady riding, and a lean sweaty horse under her; and she greeted the knight. 'Whence comest thou, my sister?' asked Peredur. She told him of the plight she was in and that journey. She was the wife of the Proud One of the Clearing. 'Aye,' said Peredur, 'I am the knight because of whom thou hast had that affliction. And he that brought it upon thee shall repent it.' And thereupon, lo, a knight coming and asking Peredur if he had seen such a knight as he was after. 'Cease thy prattle,' said Peredur. 'I am he thou dost seek, and by my faith the maiden is innocent for me.' Nevertheless they encountered, and Peredur overthrew the knight. He asked for quarter. 'Quarter thou shalt have, on condition thou return the way thou hast been, to make it known that the maiden has been found innocent, and that in her redress I overthrew thee.' The knight pledged his word thereto.

And Peredur went on his way. And on a mountain ahead of him he could see a castle. And he came towards the castle and hammered the door of the gateway with the butt of his spear. Thereupon, lo, a handsome auburn-haired youth opening the gate, in stature and girth a warrior, but in age a lad. When Peredur came into the hall, there was a big handsome woman seated in a chair, and numerous handmaidens about her. And the good lady made him welcome. And when it was time to go to meat they went. And after meat, ''Twere well for thee, chieftain,' said the woman, 'to go elsewhere to sleep.' 'May I not sleep here?' 'Nine witches, friend,' said she, 'are there here, and their father and mother with them. They are the witches of Caer Loyw. And by daybreak we shall be no nearer to escaping than to being slain. And they have overrun and laid waste the dominion save for this one house.' 'Aye,' said Peredur, 'here would I be to-night. And if trouble comes, if I can do good, that I will. Harm, however, I will not do.' They went to sleep.

And at daybreak Peredur could hear a shrieking, and quickly Peredur arose in his shirt and trousers, and his sword about his neck, and out he came. And when he came, there was a witch overtaking the watchman, and he shrieking. Peredur fell upon the witch and struck her on the head with his sword until her helm and headpiece spread like a salver on her head. 'Thy mercy, fair Peredur son of Efrawg, and the mercy of God!' 'How knowest thou, hag, that I am Peredur?' 'It was fated and foreseen that I should suffer affliction from thee, and that thou shouldst take horse and arms from me. And thou shalt be with me awhile, being taught to ride thy horse and handle thy weapons.' 'On these terms,' he replied, 'shalt thou have mercy: thy pledge that thou never do hurt to this countess's dominion.' Peredur took assurance thereof, and by leave of the countess he set off with the witch to the Witches' Court. And he was there three weeks on end. And then Peredur took his choice of horse and arms, and set out on his way.

And at the close of day he came to a valley, and at the far end of the valley he came to a hermit's cell. And the hermit made him welcome, and he was there that night. On the morrow early he arose, and when he came outside, a fall of snow had come down the night before. And a wild she-hawk had killed a duck alongside the cell, and what with the horse's clatter the she-hawk rose up, and a raven alighted

171

The Deans were offered many unsolicited books by hopeful artists, but their full programme of commissions and reprinted classics could not allow them to accept any. There was, however, one exception: Una Woodruff. Her bizarre recreations of nonexistent manuscripts appealed to their sense of mischief. The first, *Inventorum Natura*, appeared in 1979.

With a straight-faced introduction by John Michell, *Inventorum* claimed to be a long-lost manuscript of Pliny the Elder, with Una's illustrations, published for the first time to mark the nineteen-hundredth anniversary of his dramatic death in the eruption of Vesuvius. The text was in Julian Latin, meticulously "translated" by D. MacSweeney. Roger and Martyn had a lot of fun producing the book, but their greatest pleasure was receiving an angry letter from a professor of classical studies in New York denouncing *Inventorum Natura* as a forgery.

"Books to me have always been magical objects." Roger Dean takes a special delight in the illustrated books of the turn of the century: Willy Pogàny's *Parsifal*, Aubrey Beardsley's *Salome*, Arthur Rackham's *A Midsummer Night's Dream*. As well as pictures and text, they contain decorated borders, capitals and tailpieces, and are finely bound. When he became a publisher, Roger determined that one of the things he would produce would be books like these. "I wanted to possess beautiful books; rather than search for them, I thought we could make them."

A whole novel, densely illustrated and decorated throughout, represents a lot of creative effort. Roger and Martyn sought out artists and commissioned them to work on titles that attracted them. As they say: "Putting people together is as creative a process as putting together pencil and paper." The artists came from many fields: from galleries (Dick French, who illustrated J. G. Ballard's *The Drowned World*), magazines (Mike Embden, with Rider Haggard's *She*) and colleges (Sue Rowe, working on Charles Kingsley's *The Water Babies*). All these books appeared. Sadly, others did not: Marion Campbell's *The Dark Twin*, to be illustrated by Jeffrey Jones, and Thea von Harbou's *Metropolis*, on which the Fritz Lang film was based, by Michael Kaluta, are two that never reached print.

Part of the trouble was time. Projects scheduled to take eighteen months were taking twice that. There were more, intractable problems, and in many ways it was a thwarted dream. However, the last book they produced was Alan Lee's *The Mabinogion*, a suitably majestic end to a highly effective phase of operation.

MOUSE & KELLEY

chris achilleos

1977

STAR CODES

VIDEO PODS & GAMES

At the heart of Martyn Dean's design projects lies the Retreat Pod. It is big enough for one or two people to climb inside, and it provides complete privacy in the security and warmth of total enclosure.

The idea arose from an accidental experiment in isolation. Sharing an overcrowded flat as a student, Martyn retired to the space under the stairs, painted it black, pulled in a mattress, and shut the door. The resulting sensory deprivation set his imagination working. His response was not just to surrender to it, but to invent a way to use it. The result: a capsule for the exploration of personal space.

The pod was only five feet six inches by four feet six inches at its widest, but people's hesitation to shut themselves inside was swiftly overcome. Then it was difficult to coax them out. Once, a family of six was discovered happily crammed into the pod together. A feeling of well-being pervaded. Claustrophobia vanished. The broad curves of the shape were reassuring: no corners to feel trapped in.

You can equip the pod with whatever takes your fancy. The first pod, shown at the Maples/*Daily Telegraph* exhibition in 1970, contained the most advanced audiovisual equipment of the day: stereo, video, remote television cameras with an all-around view of the world outside. From darkness and silence you could move to total sensory inundation—all under your own control.

The original construction method was very quick, using plastic bubbles blown through plywood templates. "The major problem," Martyn says, "was the door. It had a huge throwout hinge, which was carefully counterbalanced. Just a touch, and the door would open smoothly and silently. It was the most complicated part of the whole design, consuming 90 percent of the manufacturing time. What makes any kind of design work is the bits you handle. Beauty we take for granted."

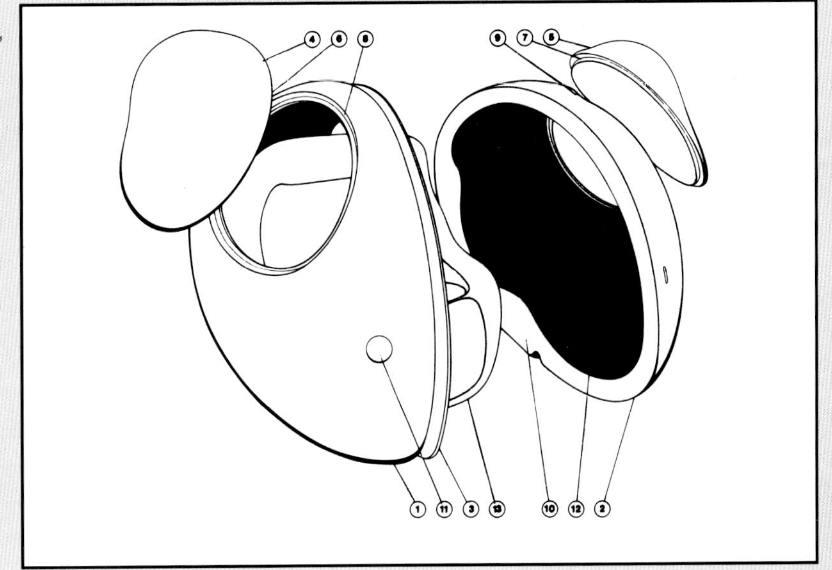

6

Plans to put the pod into production had to be shelved because of a total lack of business experience. Martyn also had to wait for the hardware to catch up with the design. In the meantime, the shape has been perfected and a new method of manu-facture devised.

Imagine the pod as private space in a public place: a hotel lobby, an office, an airport lounge. It is a facility for information or entertainment that can be kept entirely private—the telephone kiosk or public computer terminal of the future.

THE GUARDIAN

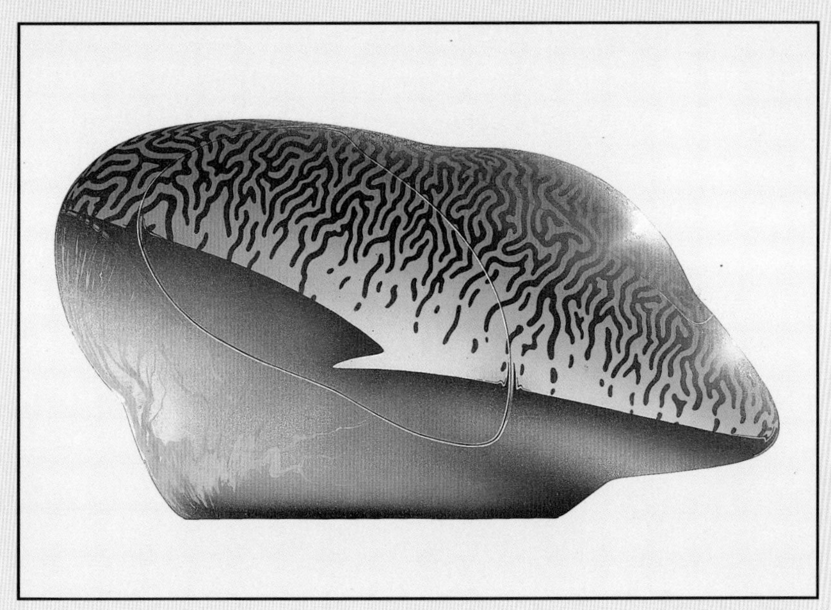

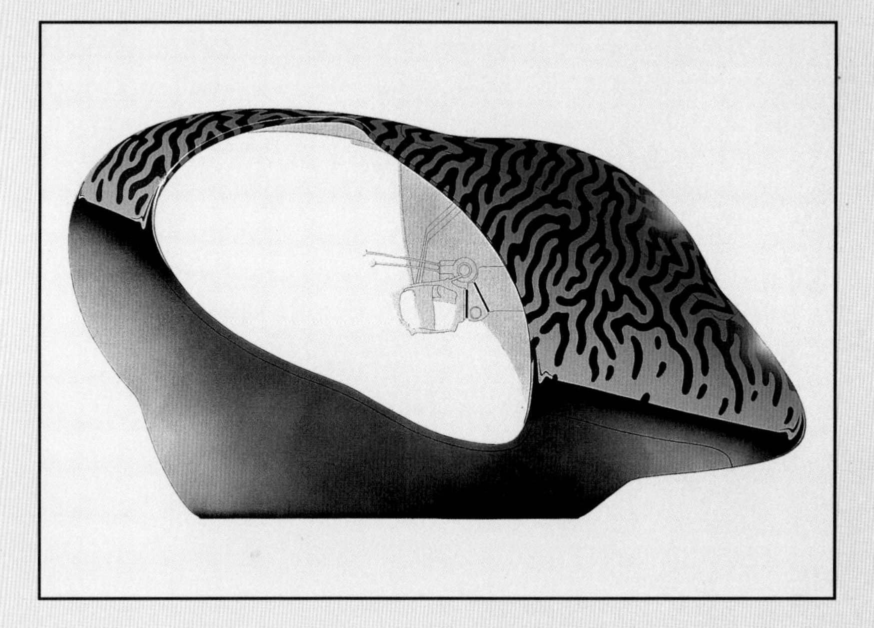

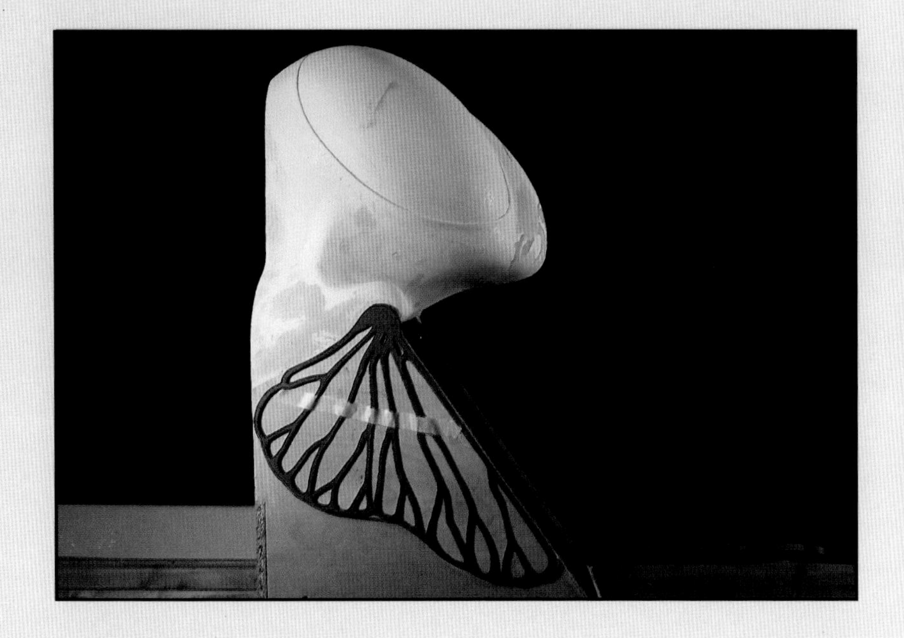

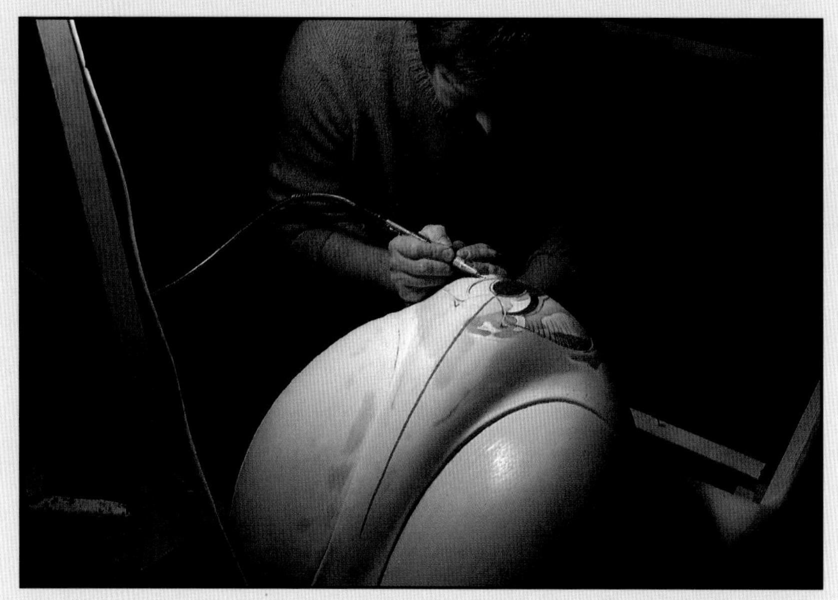

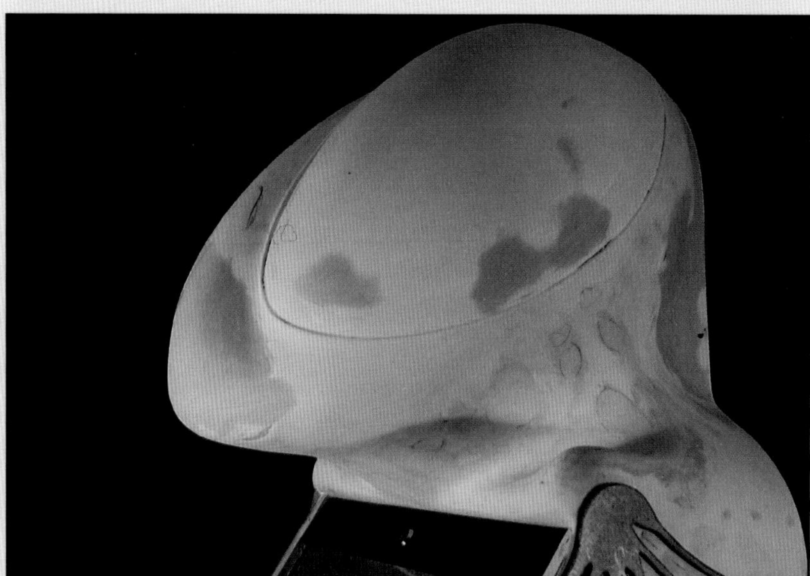

In 1980 the world was invaded by legions of creatures from outer space. Eagerly we took up their challenge and fought back. All over the country bars, arcades and service stations reverberated with electronic bleeps and crashes as volunteers queued to dispatch the alien battalions. Previously, video games were sedate: ping-pong or tennis, with a single blip batted back and forth across the screen. Suddenly they grew teeth, and the blips started to descend in infinite hordes of increasing virulence, strafing the lone defender. But if the games themselves had got smarter, their overall appearance had not.

Despite the interstellar mayhem on the screen, the video cabinets remained boring brown boxes, enlivened only with comic book flash. The Deans started work on redesigning the machines. Instead of looking like everybody's television set, wood-grained to match the living room furniture, they felt Space Invaders should look like just that—invaders from space. Martyn went for a natural image, mutated: the traditional bug-eyed monster, while Roger's creation was more belligerent, a futuristic Teutonic knight, a robot warrior.

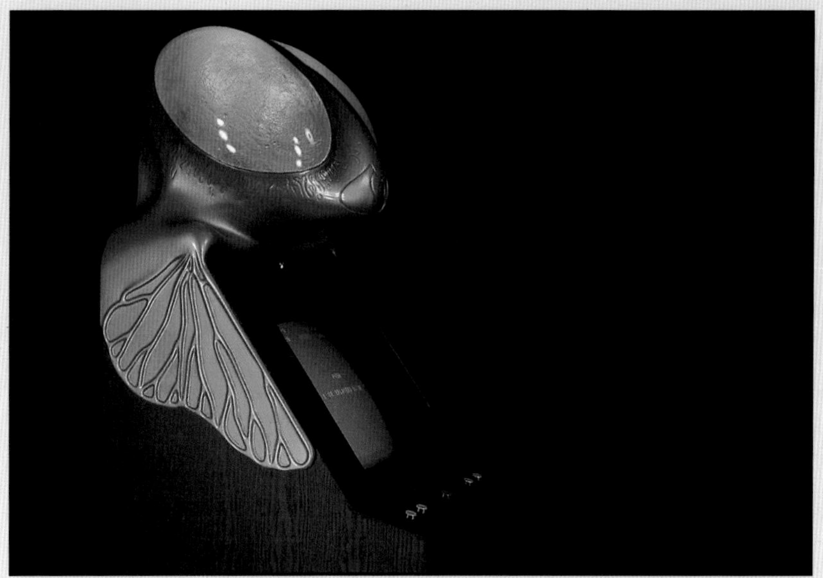

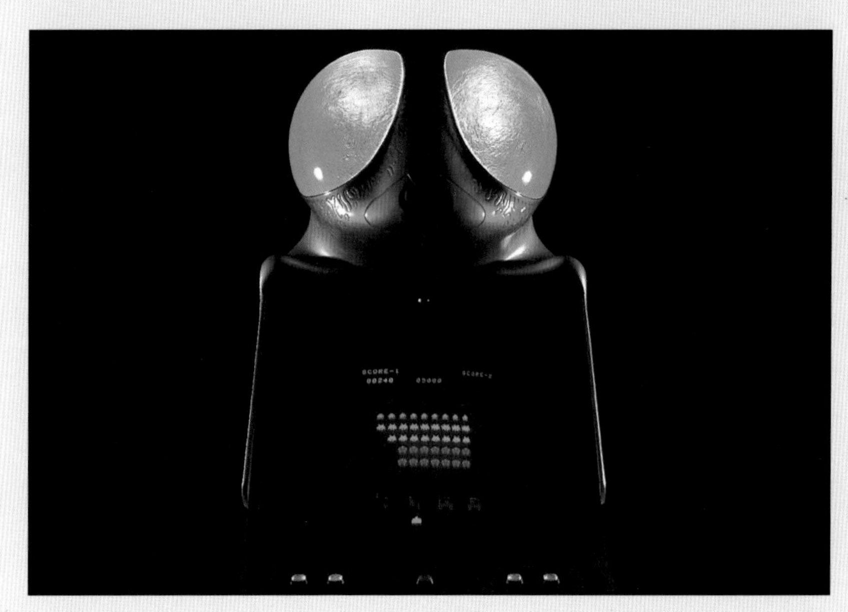

"We took the essence of what's on the video screen and put it on top of the cabinet, too, creating a sphinx," says Martyn.

At the same time, these were designs that had to work in our world. They had to survive constant use and be resistant to attacks by terrestrial vandals. The cabinet heads were RIM mouldings, made from polyurethane foam injected into moulds at high pressure, the same as modern car bumpers. The paint was also polyurethane, which bonded chemically to the surface so that it could not be chipped or scraped off.

These Space Invaders were to be distributed by Taito, so the alien heads became known as Taitans. Martyn and Roger designed them for mass production, made in two halves to fit together over the top of the machine, but gave them as much care and attention as any individual work of sculpture. The curve of the shoulder of Martyn's bug is finely turned, its wings as precisely patterned as a cicada's. All the work was accomplished to a high degree of finish, which looked like polished stone but had a metallic sheen. The eyes, polycarbonate inserts, lit up from inside. Yet all this added a mere £20 to the £1,300 the machines then cost.

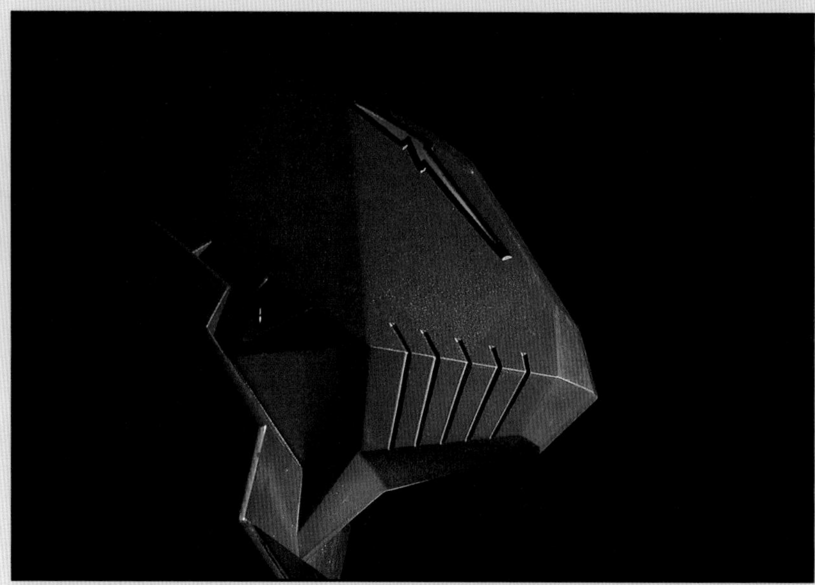

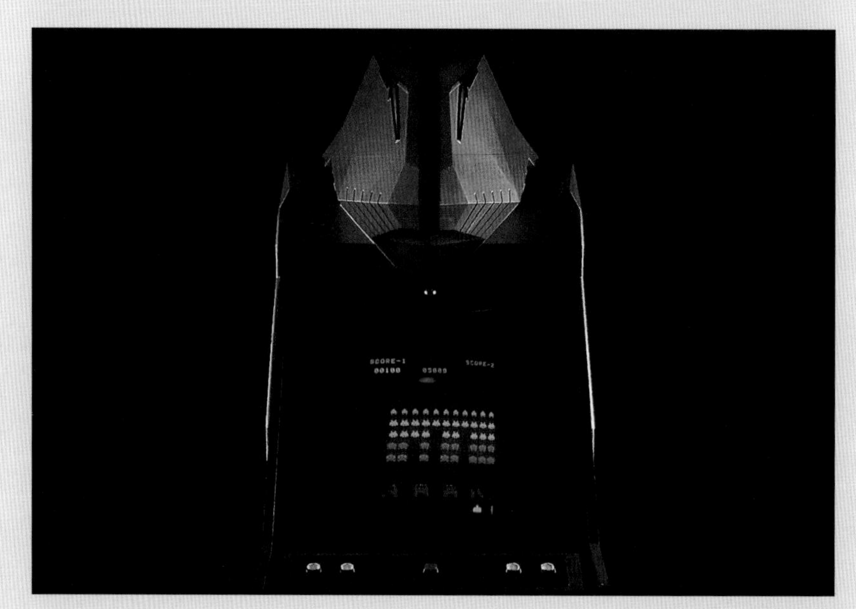

"Part of the design was the multiple factor: their appearance at attention, plugged in, ready. The lines of invaders that filled the screen also occupied the arcade: a legion shoulder to shoulder."

In search of this combined image, Martyn turned to his fascination with ancient Egypt, especially the avenues of statues at the necropolis of Karnak, guardians of the afterlife. The Karnak monuments not only took the right form, a head on a pedestal, but also had the right character. "Lined up in an arcade, the Taitans resembled a kind of intergalactic Highgate Cemetery"—memorials to a million shot-down Space Invaders.

"To research the project, we had several machines installed in the office," Martyn remembers. "Everybody became addicted and spent a frightful amount of time on them. But everybody also became ambidextrous, and productivity actually rose. When you're shot full of adrenaline it has to go somewhere, so you work like a demon."

Many amusement arcade operators come from the world of showmen and travelling fairs. Since their Taitans were also pure fairground products, Roger and Martyn were astonished when their prototypes met some resistance from the trade. They discovered that the showmen's reluctance was simply over the colour, a vivid metallic green. Showmen are enduringly superstitious, and green is unlucky. "When you venture into a new field, you must learn the local folklore, the traditions, the taboos. Even the best-planned projects can fall foul of simple cultural oversights."

Plans for mass marketing also came unstuck when Taito reorganised its most successful product and dropped the original cabinet that fitted the design. So the Deans displayed the machines themselves, in an experimental arcade that occupied a corner of their Tectonic House pavilion at a public exhibition. The bug and the robot knight stood with their humbler commercial cousins under a canopy incorporating the crystals and part of the lightning burst from Yes's Crystal stage set (see p. 54)—the first phase in a design for a total amusement environment.

ROCK STAGES

ROCK STAGE SETS 1973-1980

Stage sets by Martyn and Roger Dean are as assertive and attractive as rock music itself. Their blend of classical theatrical effects and adventurous design is pure showmanship. Imaginative exploitation of the stage space enhances and dramatises the interaction between band and audience. As always in their work, the emphasis is on appropriate environment. "The important thing," says Roger, "is that the set must be a place, where the band is playing. Not abstract, not simply decorative: a real location, definite but unknown."

The first inspiration to design stages came from the experience of Yes on tour, especially in America, where an average rock concert audience might number twenty or thirty thousand. Some of them would be sitting several hundred yards from the stage. There is not a lot to look at from that distance. At the larger open-air concerts people can be sitting as much as a quarter of a mile away, and see practically nothing. A large stage set with changing lights turns a distant glimpse into a spectacle; moving scenery adds vitality, and the closer you are, the more dramatic it becomes.

Martyn Dean's stages represent seven years' work, seven years' development from initial exploration to a peak of technical sophistication. Though entirely contemporary in conception and style, these constructions demonstrate Martyn's abiding enthusiasm for the original monumental scenery for Wagnerian opera, which needed two trains to transport it around Bavaria, and the designs for the German Expressionist cinema that followed it. Murnau's *Faust* and Lang's *Die Niebelungen* and *Metropolis* sculpted the imaginary past and future with bold angles, startling elevations, stark light and brooding shadows. For the dramatic music of Yes, Martyn projected the rock stage as a development of this school.

Led by the energetic Clive Richardson, most of the construction people labouring on the sets were art school graduates, including the two female laminators who normally turned out motorcycle components for a living and whom Martyn remembers as the two fastest-working assistants he ever hired. Artists have problems working in the unknown, and they found the challenge stimulating. Without this imaginative participation the conditions would have become intolerably rushed and uncertain. As Martyn says, "There are no points for trying hard, only for succeeding."

STAGE SET 1973-1974

The first stage set the Deans built was for Yes's *Tales from Topographic Oceans* tour in 1973–74. It was a collaboration based on Roger's design principles and philosophy. Martyn produced the finned shell that formed a pavilion for Alan White, the drummer, who found the fibreglass canopy sharpened his drum sound, making it harder, more resonant. At the climax of the "ritual" the shell opened, releasing blasts of fire and smoke. Roger contributed the illuminated islands that covered the stage and the Expressionist organ pipes that undulated in shifting colours, a visual extension of Rick Wakeman's vibrant keyboards. Roger's backdrop shaped the screen for slides and light effects.

The scheduling for this first project was sheer guesswork. There was no time to go back and start again; there never was. A frenetic, slightly unreal atmosphere prevailed. "It was fibreglass madness," Martyn recalls.

They used steel for the framework of the set because it was cheap, strong and easy to assemble, but that meant welding on site, near where buckets of violently inflammable chemicals were stored. "We were young and, thank God, eternal optimists; otherwise we'd never have taken the risks we did. But without taking risks, you never break new ground."

They soon learned that, despite the pressure of time, it was always better to stop and think a way through a problem than to keep slogging away in the hope of solving it by sheer brute labour. They had to work through the night with only coffee breaks to sustain them. Exhausted, their hands covered in fibreglass, they would doze off for a moment and wake up to find their coffee cup firmly stuck to one hand and the other hand bonded equally securely to the side of the chair.

Despairing of getting the construction properly finished in time, they sent off on tour the set of fibreglass patterns, which were solid, unwieldy and, with the steel frame, very heavy.

The set was finished and modified before it was taken to America in 1974. An illuminated tunnel was added at the centre of the stage for the band to make a dramatic entrance and exit. The idea was that the show should be a complete theatrical presentation from start to finish, just as the music was a complete entity and the performance an integration of sound and vision.

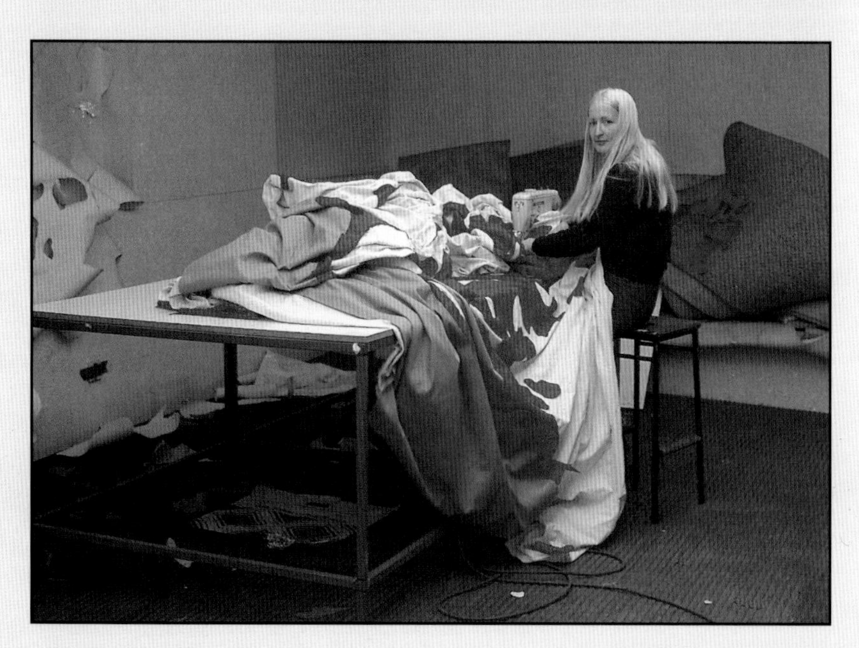

"The problem with rock 'n' roll is that everything's needed yesterday." After managing—just—to create the first Yes stage set in four months, Martyn then had to design and make the next one in three weeks before another American tour. A moving construction was therefore out of the question. He had to confine himself to the possibilities offered by the motion of lights in and around a basic shape that was itself fluid in style. He succeeded with variations on the form of a giant barnacle, which were suffused with colours that ran and changed from red to tints of aquamarine in order to resemble

the startling polychromatic displays of deep marine growths. Hollows in the barnacles collected light in pools, like sea water.

The shells were fixed in clusters along a curved platform that ran up over the drumkit and down and around behind the keyboards. Their jagged shapes were echoed in Roger's backdrop, which featured a line of sharp black rocks in silhouette, surmounted by a huge tree in green with scarlet foliage dangling. Felicity Youette had the daunting task of fixing all its shapes individually to the vast expanse of cloth.

The construction team did not get away without one final disaster. When the set was complete and painted, something was clearly wrong. It no longer looked like a clump of large and lustrous barnacles. It looked like a bunch of tulips. The paint had to be removed, and quickly, because the road crew were ready to pack the set and the plane was waiting. Twenty gallons of paint thinner were rapidly found and the barnacles washed down with it. The team were still repainting, chasing after the last of them with spray guns as they were being carried out the door.

No one could say Martyn Dean does not learn from experience. His Crystal stage for Yes in 1980 was another job with a three-week deadline from contract to delivery, and this one went like clockwork. So expert were they by now that Martyn and his team actually finished a day ahead of schedule.

The Crystal stage was used on the British tour, but the idea came in the middle of the American tour that preceded it. Martyn flew out to join the band in St. Louis and traveled with them on to Dallas. At this point all he had was a notion of something inorganic but almost animate: the imposing character of gigantic machinery, perhaps. He remembered Maloch, the mechanical god in Fritz Lang's film *Metropolis*.

"The most interesting part of this set was working for the first time in my life with straight lines and sharp edge. Everything prior to this stage set had been soft and organic in nature. This was certainly natural, but hard and crystalline.

"To keep the amount of work down, we actually made only three asymmetric moulds, yet produced an enormous variety of crystal shapes; so the geometry I had to work out was quite interesting, and entirely new."

The crystals were mounted together in two clusters, located above and behind the keyboards and drums. On the backdrop a lightning bolt flashed across the stage.

The crystals were hollow. Lit in sequence from inside, they seemed to burst out in every direction. The lightning was lurex in metallic gold, green and electric blue, appliquéd to a black velvet backdrop. The set stood twenty-two feet high and sixty wide, but it all folded up into a small chest.

"This stage synthesised all we'd learned about packing. In the past we'd manufactured frames in steel tubing, which was awkward for the road crew to handle. This time we used a complete system of lightweight, snap-together aluminum scaffolding with clip-on braces, which they could use for storing gear and climbing on. We fitted casters to everything, and carrying handles to everything else. The whole thing was very easy to operate.

"Like the Barnacle set, the Crystal did not move but had great presence. For sheer dynamism, I made the 1976 stage the Crab."

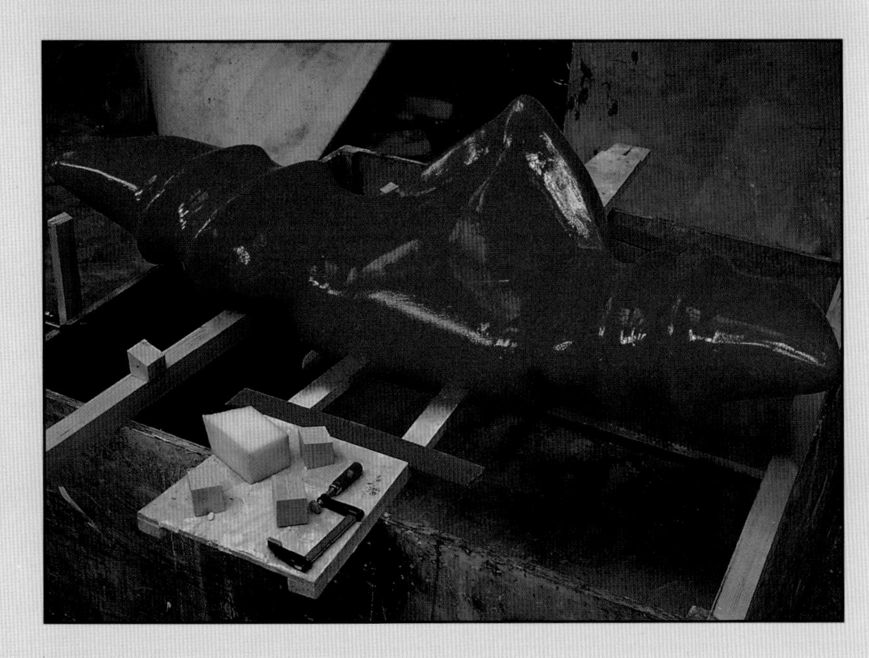

The music of Yes is spacious; it evokes landscapes. Some passages are stark and rocky, others pastoral and rolling. You can hear the pounding waters, the leaping fires; see the clear stars overhead. The life that breathes that rich atmosphere must be powerful but mysterious.

The three-headed crab loomed over the band, gazing down. Its blood was electric, its eyes beacons in the throbbing night. It lived on music. It nested in light.

This stage moves: unfolding, rising and falling rhythmically. Light bursts within the central body, suspended like a turtleshell above the drumkit. The light flows, pulsating, up and along three giant spines. Together, three heads rise and blazing eyes sweep across the audience. Its presence is awesome, its power titanic; yet it responds to the music, dancing.

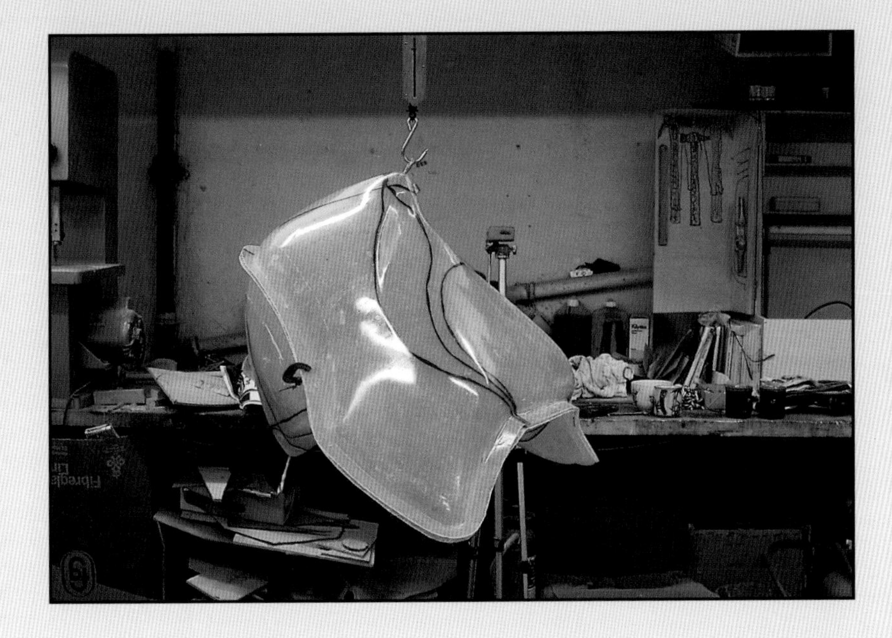

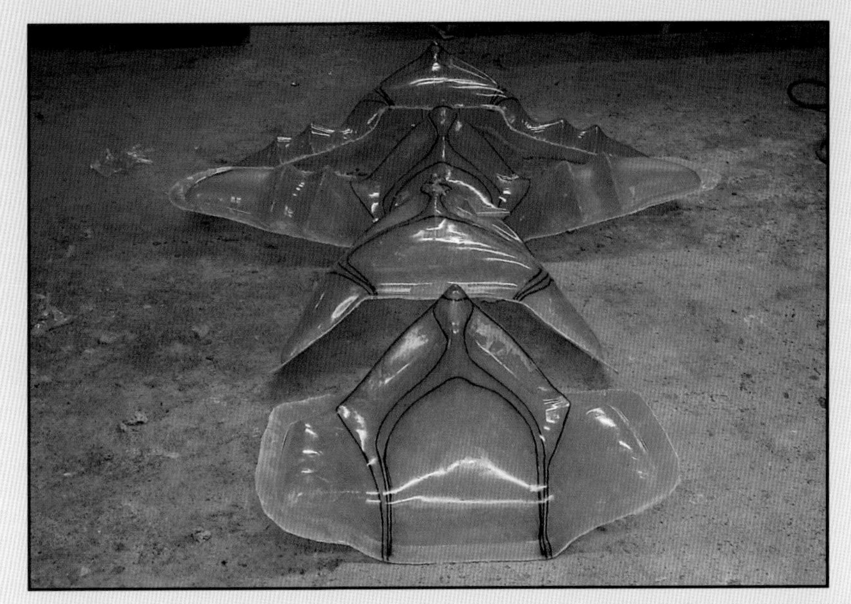

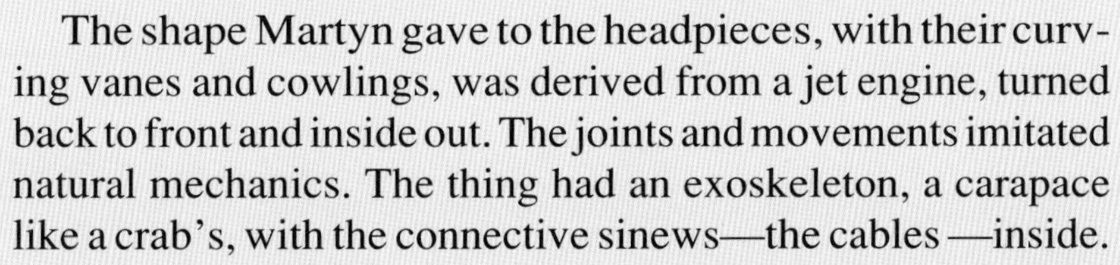

The shape Martyn gave to the headpieces, with their curving vanes and cowlings, was derived from a jet engine, turned back to front and inside out. The joints and movements imitated natural mechanics. The thing had an exoskeleton, a carapace like a crab's, with the connective sinews—the cables —inside.

The stage design, as always, worked from the unknown to the unknown. Martyn went straight to the workshop, with no designs or drawings. Taped on the wall was his list of key words and phrases including: *White Shock, Electric Blue, Intangible Technology, Beams, Biological Engineering, Hydrostatic*.

Everything that was built expanded out of these; and everything was checked back, at every phase of construction, to make sure all those concepts were present. When you are building a machine that has never been built before, there are no plans; and when you come up against a problem, there is no reference book. Instead Martyn had his list of words, a cryptic map.

Everything they needed was invented on the spot and put into production straight away. Moulds were made from plywood ribs and slats, covered with flexible foam, then plaster sealed with shellac varnish. The technique itself was rapid, each form taking little more than a week to make, but the whole job required ten people working flat out for three months. Martyn himself often put in an eighteen-hour day. Manipulating unorthodox shapes that were to do unorthodox jobs, under the punishing conditions of a long American tour, he had to improvise treatments and techniques at every turn. The finished construction would house most of the stage lighting, so resins had to be mixed that would be heat-proof, fireproof and shatterproof and still be transparent.

In the early days the construction was all black and white. To seal the patterns with ordinary brown shellac was too depressing. Martyn had them sprayed with bright pink shellac imported from Paris. "It was really startling," he says. "It brought us all back to life."

Working through the depths of winter, they taped themselves into disposable paper boiler-suits for protection against an amazing assortment of chemicals and powdered glass. The cheapest disposable headgear they could find was from a joke shop, so for days everyone walked around in bowlers or caps with cats' ears. It was so cold that resins would have taken thirty-six hours to set, so great quantities of catalyst were used. Any chance-neglected bucket of resin could suddenly shatter or melt silently into a steaming, noxious puddle.

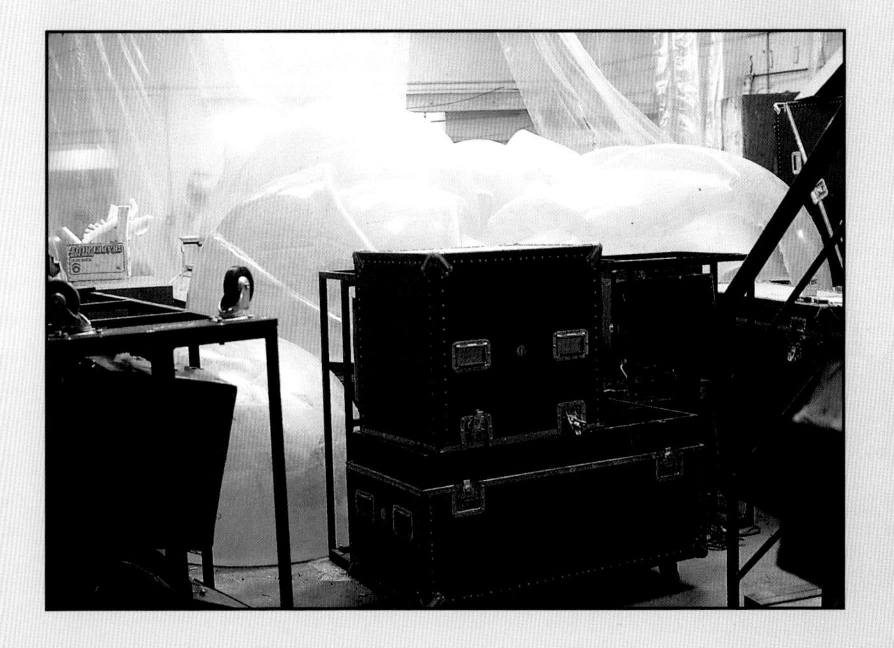

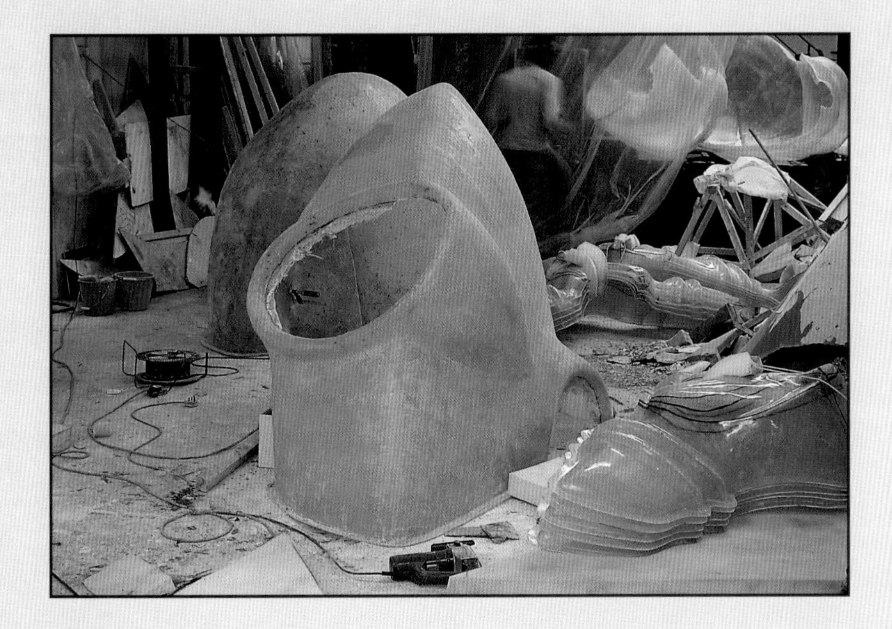

When the moulds were finished, Martyn took them to a fibreglass manufacturer he found in the Yellow Pages. "That's the first and last time I ever made that mistake. At the end of the week I went round, and instead of having made six mouldings he'd only made one, and it was awful, full of air bubbles. And I'd partly paid him already! Fortunately the man was so idle, not only had he not done the work, he hadn't even banked the money. He didn't protest too much when we cancelled the job and took back all our materials."

"You can't compound error with procrastination." Martyn and his crew set to, and the rest of the manufacture went smoothly enough, though a few adjustments had to be made. The individual vertebrae of the alien crab's three spines were laced with carbon fibres for strength, but this made them too rigid. Because these sections had to carry heavy-duty cable up to the aircraft landing lights in the nose cones, as well as for the stage lighting, they eventually were mounted on interlocking aluminum A-frames, like bicycles. A number of spare fibreglass units were taken along on the tour, just in case. It is a tribute to the success of the design that none of them was needed.

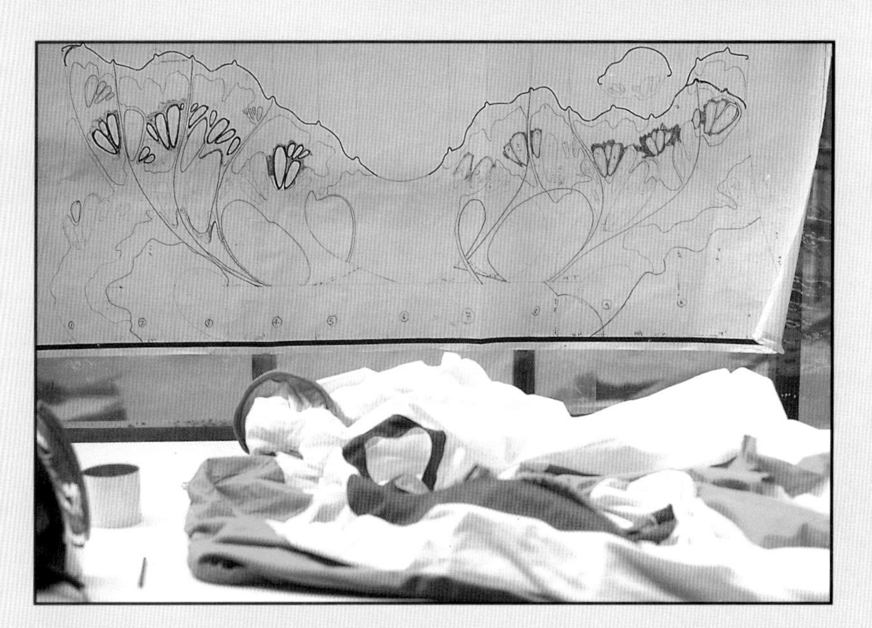

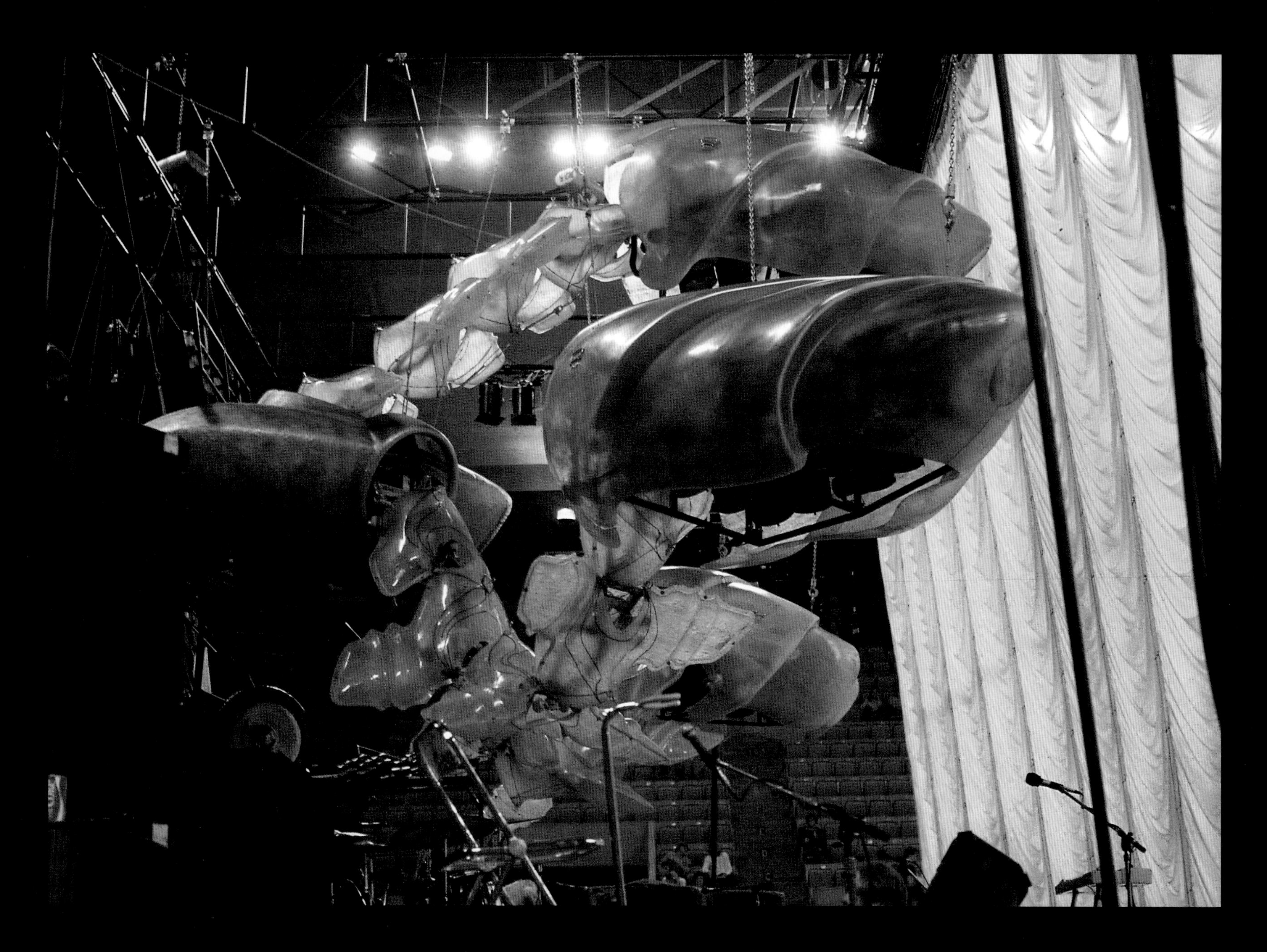

The effect of the finished stage was so impressive, the illusion of an alien technology so complete, that it is easy to overlook the practicalities of putting something so complex on tour at all. It is not only what the set looks like on the stage that matters, it is how it travels, how it fits into the back of a truck. The road crew are going to be moving it every day for several months, and anything that does not work is soon going to be smashed. Loading a truck after a gig is a high-speed art. To transport the linked vertebrae, special cradles had to be constructed from aluminum ladders and nylon webbing.

With three chain-hoists to each head and each vertebra rolling forward over the one beneath as the heads rose, the illusion of monstrous movement was complete. Assembling everything for the first time in an empty American stadium, Martyn at last saw his machine perform. It worked first time, without a squeak, without a wobble. After months of hell and scepticism came triumph, and a round of applause from a nearby gang of stevedores. "That's the highest accolade you can get in this business."

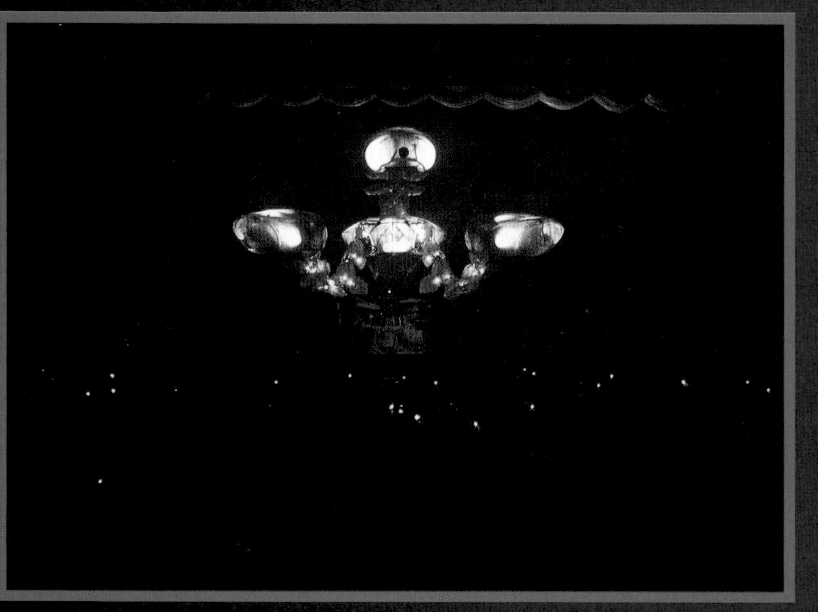

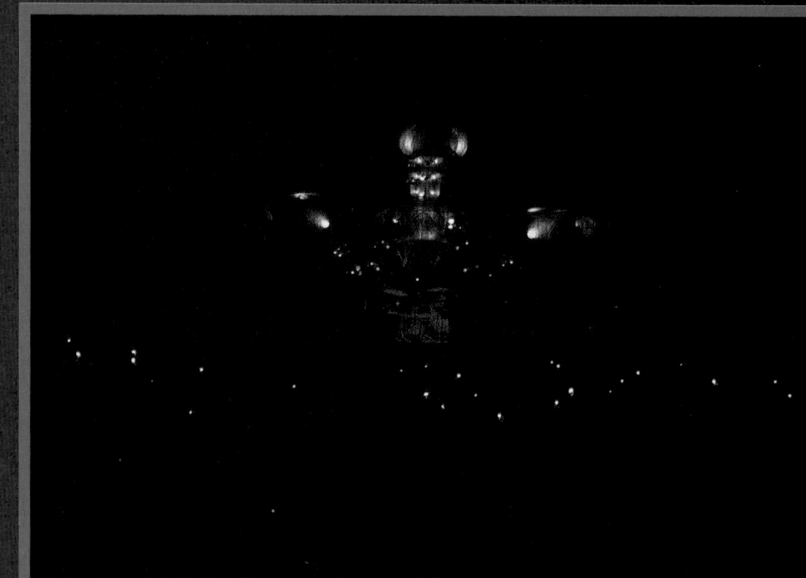

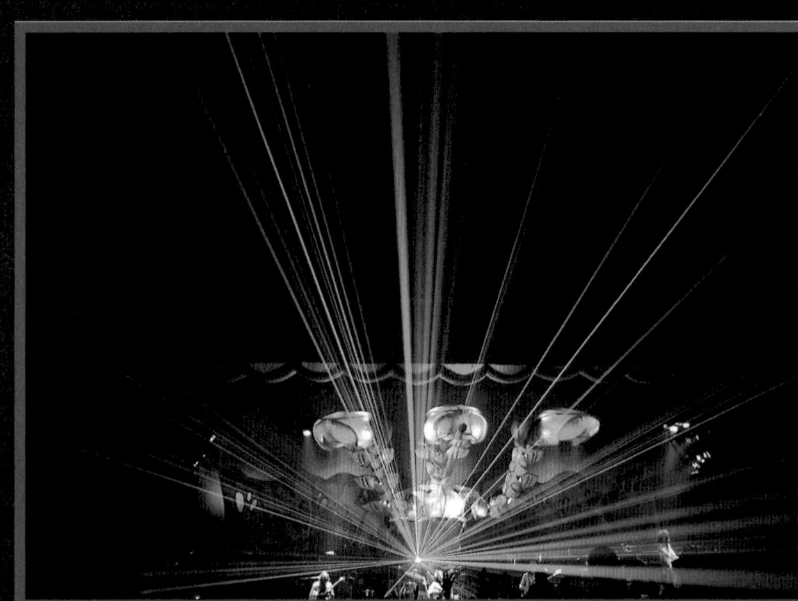

Although on tour the lighting and special effects were controlled and operated by the band's engineers, all the movements first had to be choreographed: machine, lights, lasers, dry ice. For this Martyn returned to the list of key words from his workshop, checking the elements as each moved into place. When the internal lights went out, the set disappeared. "Anything that's onstage for three hours becomes boring if you can't make it vanish." Through the glassy shapes loomed the marbled backdrop designed by Roger and made by Felicity Youette, the cloth suspended like a tent from two giant coat hangers. Everything there was scenery, a setting for the band, but scenery raised to the level of the spectacular.

The show begins, darkness glimmering. The alien machine hugs the floor, waiting. In the auditorium thousands of little flames appear, every hand holding up a burning match or lighter. As if in answer to these votive sparks, the central pod begins to glow. Light pulses up through the vertebrae as the heads stir and lift. Searchlights sweep through space, and Yes materialise, while above them the organic machine basks on smoky beams of light.

ALBUM COVERS

The world of Roger Dean is as complete and tangible as our own. In fact, his world *is* our own, redesigned by a more generous and tolerant imagination. Mountains sprout like mushrooms. Boulders float. Lakes fly. Below, the buildings, from simple domestic houses to gigantic castle-cities, are moulded comfortably to the contours of the earth. There is space to move and time to grow. At dawn the light breaks warm and clear, and dragons dance in the sky.

And Roger's world is entirely real to him. "There I'm on my home ground," he says. In his mind it is all planned, all fully grown. Within this imagined world he knows exactly where to find what he needs. Each painting is a window, a different point of view. Ideas seem to come instantaneously, though it is impossible to say how long they have been germinating. Within an hour he will have a thumbnail sketch; then comes the hard work.

"It's manual effort that makes the picture. Very early on, when I was at art school, I realised the real trick was to put in incredibly long hours on what's actually a very boring process." Roger plays tapes to divert his attention—speech and drama rather than music: "It isn't distracting enough." With his mind occupied, his hand is free to work.

His chosen media are transparent watercolours for the cooler, fainter background tones and shellac inks for foreground and sky. Normally he builds up the picture area by area, but recent projects have sent him to investigate other techniques and materials that promise new developments in the future.

When it appeared on Steve Howe's first solo album, and in the closing pages of *Views, Beginnings* included a photograph of Steve standing in the white doorway surrounded by his guitars. As usual, Roger conceived the illustration as a two-dimensional compression of a three-dimensional design idea: a music room, something he might build one day. Characteristically, though the setting appears to be a rocky landscape, everything in the picture is actually indoors, within the structure of a house that contains its own water garden.

Steve's photograph does not appear on the accompanying poster because sometime after the painting had been delivered to Atlantic Records, someone put down a cup of coffee right in the middle of it. The painting itself was waterproof and robust, but the photographic montage was ruined.

For Steve's second record, *The Steve Howe Album*, in 1979, Roger painted another architectural marvel built in the same style. This time you cannot see that it is a building at all from the front of the sleeve as the picture appears to show only an indistinct figure swimming in a rock pool.

The swimmer has since disappeared as Roger was not altogether satisfied with the figure. "I put it in because I thought it added to the strangeness of the picture. When I showed it to Steve he was very kind about it, so I left it in. Finally I decided I couldn't stand it, so I took it out; and then Steve admitted he hadn't really liked it either."

Inhabited or not, the pool seems ordinary enough. It is only when you examine the back of the sleeve and see the metallic structure supporting the whole thing high up in the sky that you realise what you thought were the reflections of rocks in the pool are actually the bottoms of the rocks themselves. It is a ring of bright water, suspended in space.

The terrain of Roger's paintings is often ambiguous, but always perfectly clear. "When I'm painting a rock, I'm painting a rock. I don't want it to be a vague impression of a rock; that rock has got to look solid, as if you could pick it up. If I used a loose, sketchy technique, people would think the ambiguity was a consequence of that technique. I wanted it to be quite definite: this is a lake, but a lake that has no bottom. You're looking straight through it into the sky. I felt I had to use a technique that was as hard as possible. Something photographic would be best of all, because then the slightly surreal quality would be most effective."

The Flights of Icarus was a further evolution of the same idea. It, too, shows a rock pool in the sky, this one held together by the roots of a wonderfully windswept and twisted tree.

"I really enjoyed doing these islands in the sky. Everyone knows what it would feel like to float, to fly at will. Everyone's had a hint of that, a memory of a dream."

Roger painted this picture for an anthology of fantasy art published by Paper Tiger. Donald Lehmkuhl provided a lyrical text. "Now, a boy falls out of the Sun. Beneath, the burning sea. The Universe is tumbling through his head."

The original painting was as it appears here, without a figure. The diving boy was added only for the cover of the anthology (see p. 22). Feathers from his melted wings drift among the words of the title above him. Perhaps he is the missing swimmer from Steve Howe's sky-pool.

Though the circle of rocks in *Icarus* is floating freely, the pool itself suggests security and permanence through the presence

of the ancient tree, the grass growing in the crevices. *Pathways*, on the other hand, is decidedly insecure. There is a sense of vertigo here as the composition leads your eye down a faltering spiral staircase.

Pathways was produced as the cover for an album by John Lodge. The record's title was *Natural Avenues*, but Roger and Martyn Dean decided on a picture of a very unnatural avenue indeed. They collaborated on this sleeve, with an image they had shared for a long time. It was Martyn who came up with the idea of an avenue in the sky, proposing to treat it as a photomontage. He already had a file of pictures taken from aeroplane windows on various trips. Now he chartered a small plane at Blackbushe Airport and made several flights, hunting for a dramatic cloudscape. "We always had a tendency to do far more research than was strictly necessary."

But even with such a wealth of material, it was difficult to find photos of a path and a sky that worked well together. Roger was already designing the lettering, so now he took on the task of painting the avenue in the clouds. Martyn suggested adding the stepping stones that spiral up and down, "from an old dream, a dream of walking down a staircase that falls away into the void."

As Martyn and Roger pursued the image through several other sky scenes, included as a booklet inside the album, the idea became more and more refined until it was just a disconnected line of stones drifting in space.

Pathways is one of the few original Dean designs to have gone missing, but not even the disappearance of the artwork could put an end to that tantalising image. Years later, arranging a landscape around their Tectonic House exhibit (p. 144), Martyn suspended a truckload of fibreglass boulders in the air, bemusing all the spectators.

Yesshows, released in 1980, was the first live Yes recording in seven years. In the meantime the band had had two album covers designed by Hipgnosis. For this one they came back to Roger. His first idea was to do something entirely new, and he offered the lettering for the title *Yes Indeed!*, a complete change of tone, and quite a suitable name for a live album. The band preferred *Yesshows*. Because live albums draw on previous work as reinterpreted onstage, Roger also looked back, to *Yessongs* and the story of the mushroom rocks told in its four-picture gatefold.

The finished cover, in Roger's opinion, is not one of his most successful works, though the composition is effective enough. Again he chose to disguise what he was doing, with an innocent-seeming front cover: a snowy rockscape against grey and purple mists. The bird originally was only in the title logo, and was added to the sky later for a flash of colour. ("The creatures in my pictures lead such unstable lives.")

On the back of the sleeve the viewpoint shifts. The bird has flown and the mists are parting to disclose a familiar looming shape, while the foreground rocks are revealed as the roof of a Dean Tectonic House, this one simultaneously an underground warren and another of his buildings in the sky.

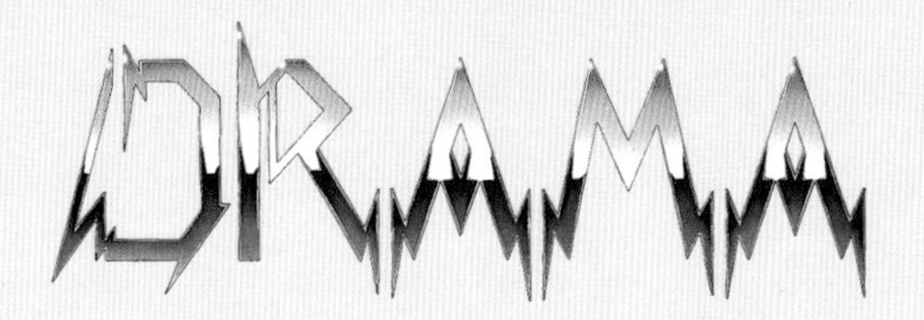

Roger worked with Yes once more, in 1980. The band had a new lineup, with Geoff Downes and Trevor Horn replacing Rick Wakeman and Jon Anderson. A new visual style was called for and, first, a new Yes logo. Roger experimented with hard-edged, jagged lettering, but eventually decided to maintain continuity by keeping the curved shape and expressing the new approach with a change of colouring. Previously the three letters had been filled in with toned colour, a different one for each album. The new metallic look made the logo appear three-dimensional, sculpted in silver or formed from mercury. An angular letterface was drawn for the album title, *Drama* (see p. 54).

Rogercontinued in the new direction with his cover painting. "It's quite out of line with what I'd done before: not part of that early Yes sequence, a different landscape, though still with a strange feel to it. Because I'd had difficulty with *Yesshows*, I though I'd reinvestigate that stormy sky. I thought, 'I can do a much better job than that'; and I did!"

At first Roger followed his normal practice of painting sky and foreground in shellac ink and the background in watercolour, but the slanting rocks turned out much too dark for the contrast. He had to sponge the watercolour off until he recovered the brightness he wanted.

That was not the only change the picture went through. Originally there was a settlement in the middle distance, a village or camp with lights shining in the darkness. "I didn't like it. Nobody else did either, though everybody liked the structure of the picture."

Because both shellac and watercolours are transparent, the only way to paint out the settlement was with gouache, a medium Roger very rarely used. He replaced it with the lake and boulders and, mysteriously, two wrecked ships. The hull of one and the superstructure of the other are quite visible but frequently go unnoticed.

The scene has an atmosphere of desertion, but none of the unearthly quality of *Close to the Edge* or *Relayer*. The bizarre growths at the left in the foreground are a form of cacti, which fascinate Roger: plants as sculpture. The three black cats chasing two white birds were painted last, to add movement and narrative to the scene. "Landscape, or landscape with architecture—that's what I like doing. Sometimes it's necessary to bring it to life, to add something living, and plants alone don't do the job. It needs something dynamic: a dragon, an eagle, cats—or even people." These occasional elements put more in the picture than can actually be seen, encourage you to surmise what has just happened or what is just about to.

Immediately after *Drama* Yes split up. Roger had stayed in touch with Steve Howe, so he knew he was forming a new band, to be called Asia. He even sketched one or two logos for them, but they wanted something quite different. They told him it was important that nobody should think they were trying to be Yes II. After a while Roger came back to them with a new logo, simple, geometric and distinctive.

When he came to paint the cover for their debut album, Roger knew straight away the image he wanted: a heraldic Chinese dragon, lithe and moving fast, but seen frozen at the instant of splashing down on a dark sea in pursuit of a shining sphere. The complex, dynamic composition took him thirty or forty sketches to resolve. "It had to have the energy of a whiplash, yet fit the form exactly and still be convincing naturalistically."

This dragon is not a sea serpent but a beast of the air, caught between sky and water in dramatic sunlight against black clouds. The sphere it chases is the Pearl of Wisdom, completing an allegorical reference to Chinese mythology. Some people have claimed to find the name "Asia" in the pyramidal form of the dragon's coils, but this is just a happy coincidence. At nearly four feet by three, the painting is one of Roger's largest.

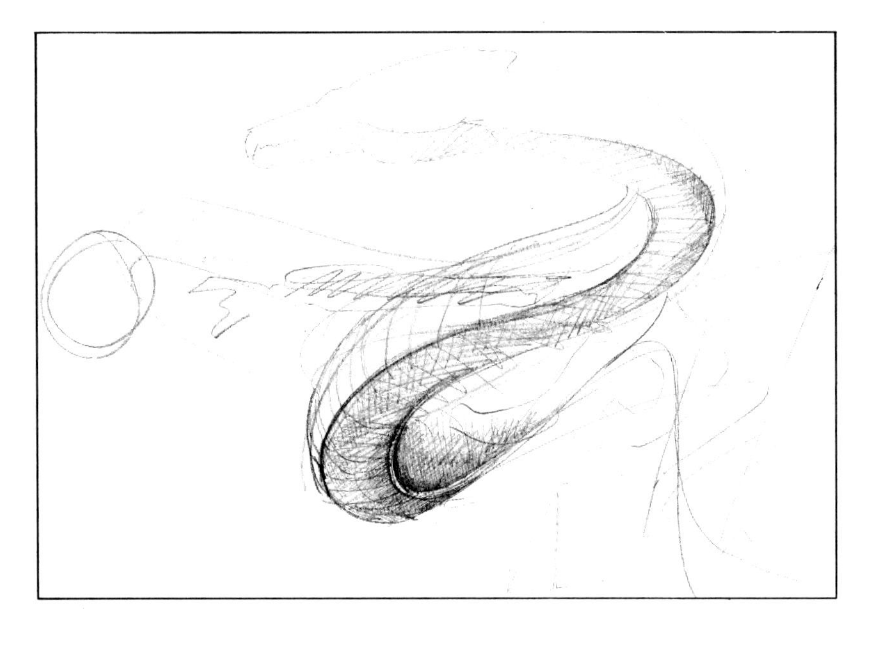

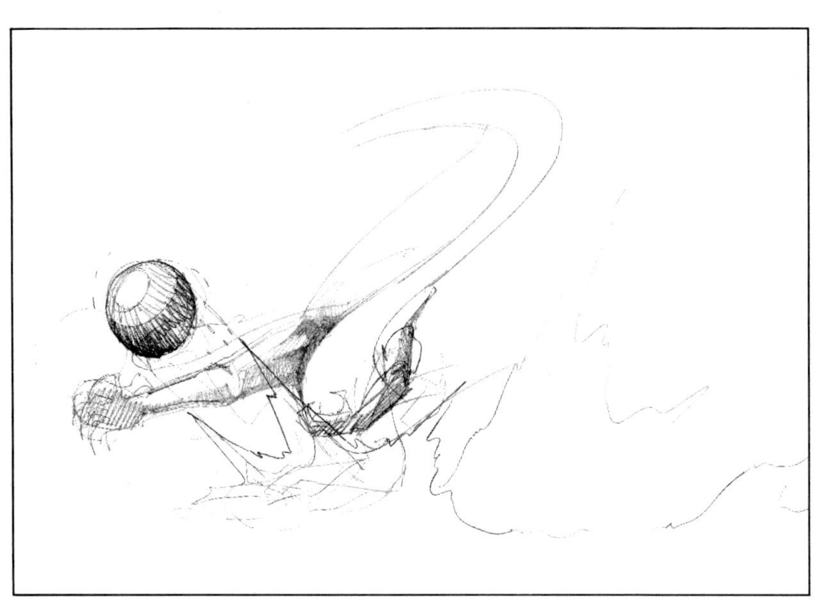
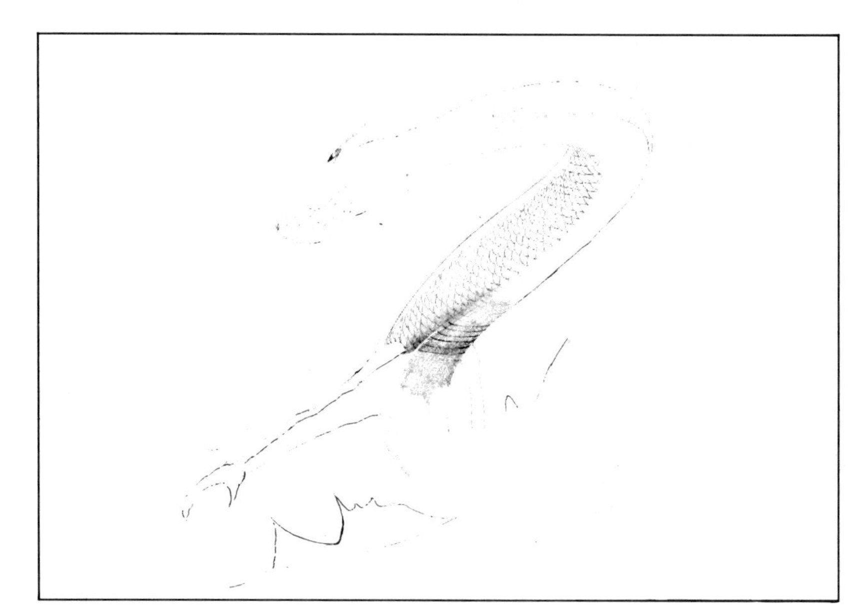

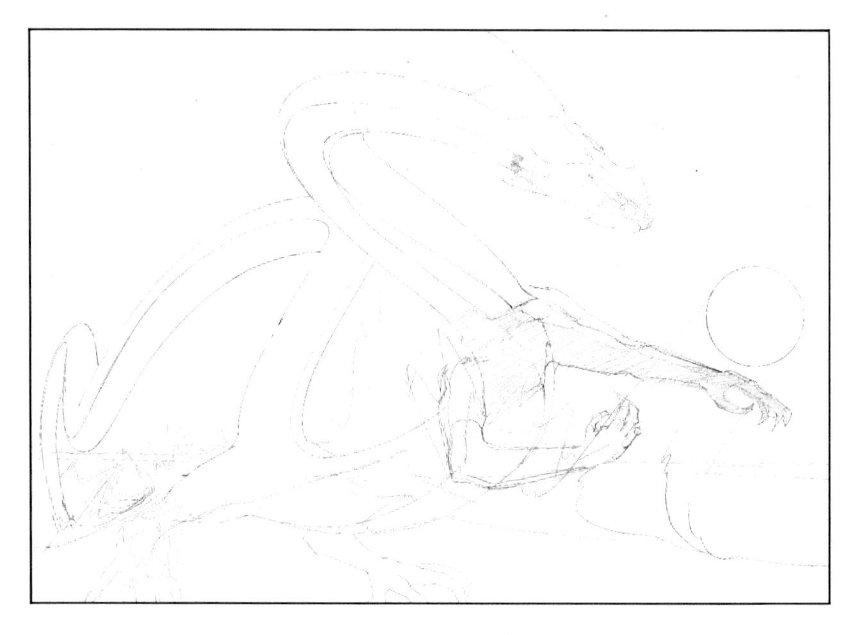

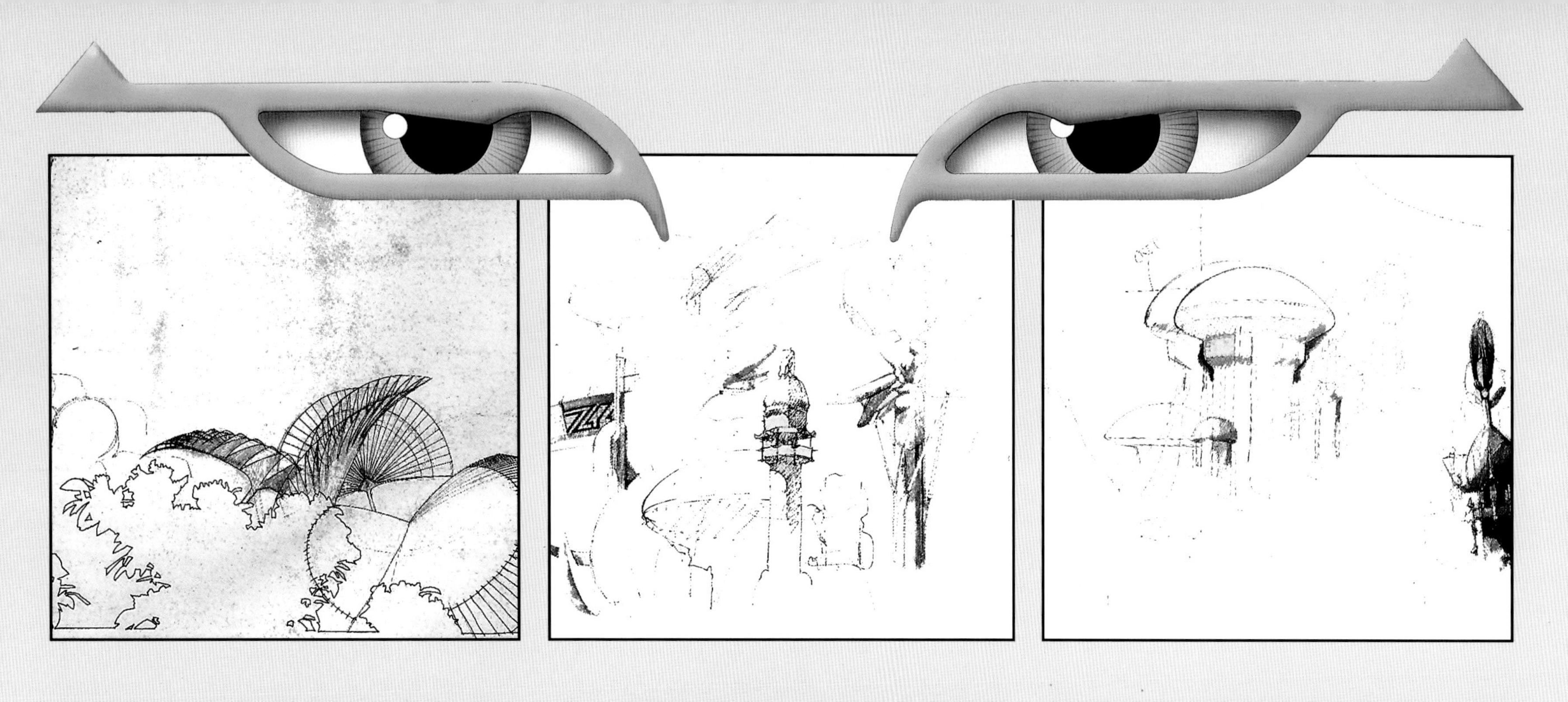

Collecting ideas from his sketchbook for Asia's second album, *Alpha*, Roger took five to show the band. Everybody liked a different one. Roger's own favourite showed Chinese fan palms, with tigers hidden in their shadows; but John Wetton preferred one of a fish-eagle attacking a diving fish. Carl Palmer chose a scene of domed towers, futuristic in outline but closely ornamented in Asian styles, with Persian tiling or Chinese gargoyles. Geoff Downes voted for a sphinx and the domed towers.

The sketch Steve Howe liked was an idea of Martyn's, a pyramid with eyes. Ten miles from Kathmandu, Martyn had come upon a Buddhist monument called Boudnathe Stupa, and taken an extraordinary photograph of it. The stupa has a dome with a stepped pyramid above it, a golden canopy above that, and around the base of the pyramid four pairs of eyes stare sternly out to the four corners of the earth: the eyes of Buddha.

What Roger eventually made was a scene from the imaginary Orient suggested by the band's name, overlaying the images like slides in a magic lantern. Vast in the distance rises the pyramid; before it, the towers, on the far bank of a jungle river. The tigers lurk in the foreground foliage; behind them falls the eagle. Only the sphinx has slouched off out of sight. Roger decided to reduce the decoration on the towers to give prominence to the eyes of the pyramid. Experiments with designs based on Martyn's photographs taught Roger the trick of Buddha's frown: the dip in the upper eyelids narrows and concentrates the gaze. He painted a pair of Asiatic eyes, halfway between Egyptian and Tibetan, and six feet across. He tried out their effect by fixing them to the wall and letting them stare at him.

Roger had planned to have the eyes appearing everywhere—in shop windows, on buses, as car stickers—as well as on the album cover itself and on every page of the 1983 tour programme. But before the tour was properly underway the second half had to be cancelled. The band returned to Britain and Greg Lake joined for a short Japanese tour.

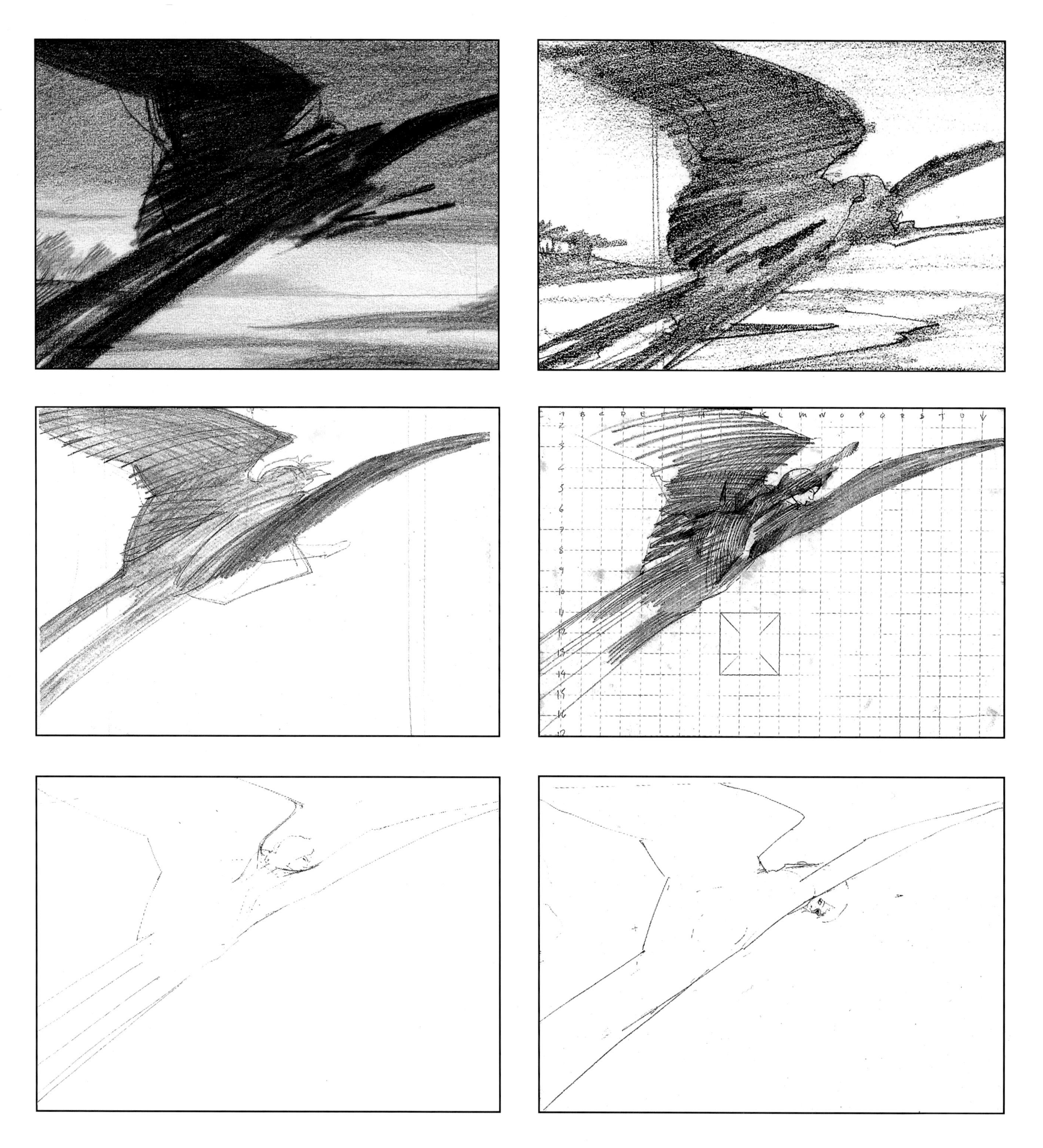

NIGHT
WINGS

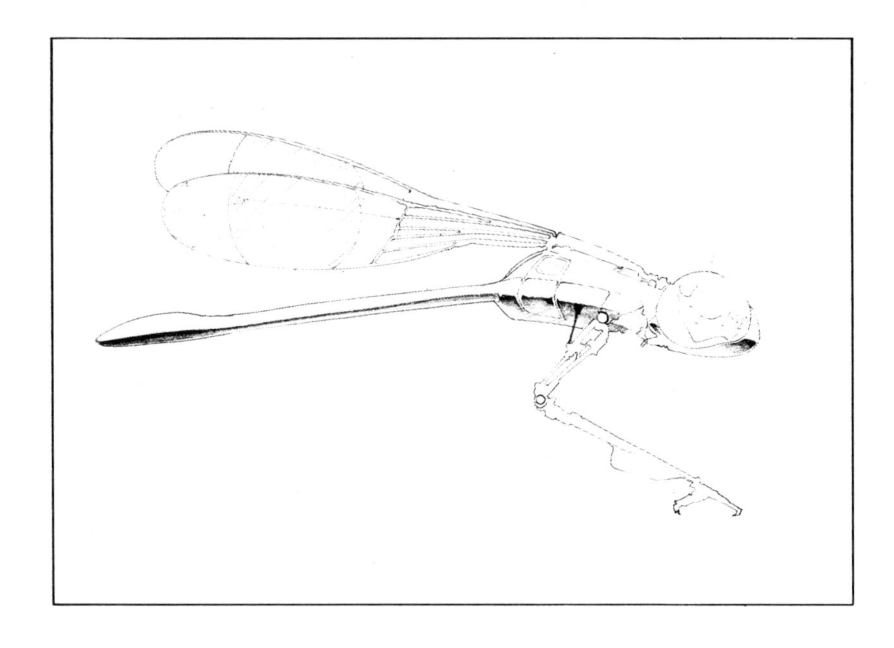

Over the years Roger has often been approached by people with animation projects. Most have little interest for him, but a television advertisement for Sony audiocassettes fitted in with what he prefers to work on: not the animation itself but the scenery, the environment. The agency asked him to paint a long background and design mechanical creatures for their animators to bring to life. They wanted him to illustrate the sort of music he was associated with, and as Roger understood that Yes would be providing the soundtrack, it was obvious that the recognisable Yes iconography was what was required. He therefore put together a painting that quoted from *Close to the Edge, Yessongs, Drama* and *Classic Yes.*

Roger finished the painting very fast, in one weekend, using only shellac inks because watercolours were too delicate for television studio conditions. Instead of working area by area, he did all the blue first (cobalt) for maximum depth, and then added red (magenta) and yellow. Seeing that it might be difficult for other people to animate his very detailed style, he produced storyboards with the cats from *Drama* as black silhouettes, which could easily be made very lifelike. This suggestion was not taken up. The animators had exactly the problems he had anticipated, and produced simplistic creatures that looked wooden rather than mechanical. To make matters more confusing, the music was not by Yes but by Godley and Creme.

Morning Dragon (frontispiece) captures one complete narrative moment: a dragon at play in the early sunlight of some mythic Oriental morning. "I was looking for a feeling of exhilaration, of leaping around in the sky."

Although this looks like a single painting, it is actually a montage of several elements. The dragon itself was originally drawn on its own, in black ink, and subsequently coloured and put into the landscape. The sky is poster paint, airbrushed (a new departure for Roger), and the rocks are gouache, a medium chosen for its flat, opaque, pastel effect. The rocks in stronger colours on the left were marbled and then painted out to near black. The roses and the bee in the snail shell were first done for a Yes sleeve, *Tales from Topographic Oceans*, but never used. Roses, bee and dragon were cut out and carefully stuck down on the background.

The montage was made with a book project in mind, *The Dragon Almanac*, with Donald Lehmkuhl, but before the work could be completed, the bookshops were suddenly inundated with dragon books, and the project was shelved. This dragon, however, has appeared in several places since: on the cover of a dragon calendar for 1979, repainted as a logo and letterhead for Magnetic Storm, and as a line drawing in Roger's contribution to a Japanese poster art exhibition.

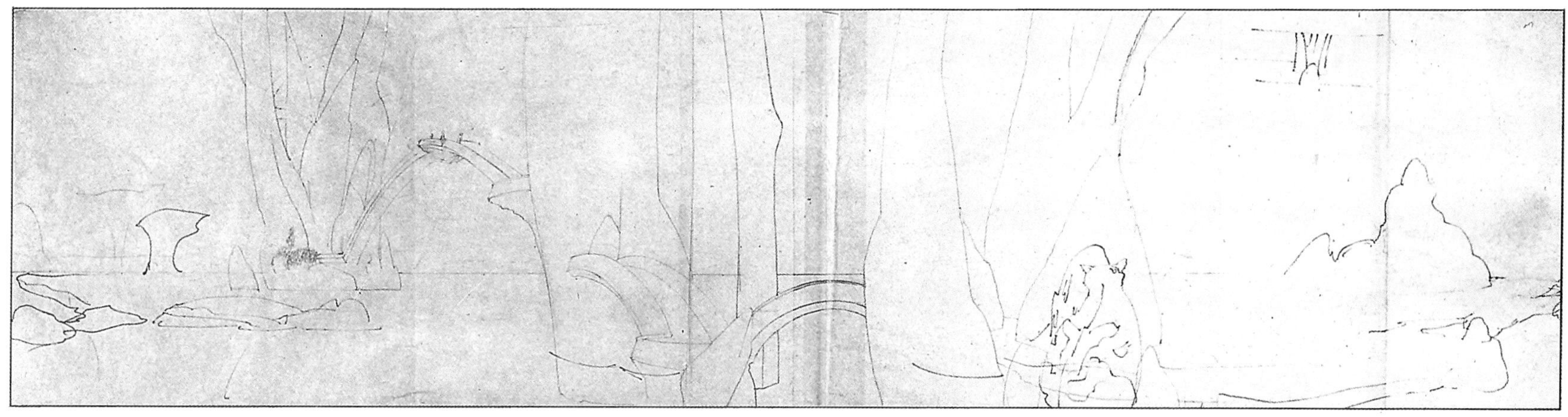

THE WAR OF THE WORLDS

THE
WAR
OF THE
WORLDS

First published in 1898, H. G. Wells's *The War of the Worlds* continues to tower over science fiction as the Martian fighting machines themselves did over the devastated English countryside. When Jeff Wayne was planning a musical interpretation of the book in 1977, he asked Roger to paint him a record cover. Roger suggested a combined book and record album, a format that was to succeed later for Wood-roffe and Greenslade's *The Pentateuch* (see p. 22). The contractual procedures were too complex to resolve at this earlier attempt, so Jeff and Roger went their separate ways.

The Magnetic Storm project based on *The War of the Worlds* was many-faceted. To make the most of it, it was decided to involve other artists, the best in their respective fields. Tim White, renowned for his science fiction hardware paintings, and Richard Clifton-Dey were commissioned to produce a series of a dozen pictures from Roger's designs. Meanwhile, in consultation with Martyn, Roger started to draw Martian tripods that could actually be built for a stage show. This was quite a challenge, for though H. G. Wells had described the machines vividly enough to chill readers for the best part of a century, he had not written instructions for engineers.

A tripod is perfectly stable on uneven ground, but once it starts to move it is unbalanced. A previous attempt to model Wells's Martians, for Byron Haskin's 1953 film, had overcome the problem by cheating—replacing the tripods with flying saucers. A three-legged thing is potentially far more frightening because, as Martyn Dean points out, it is completely alien. On Earth, no living creature has legs in anything but pairs. Nevertheless, he and Roger came up with a design

that looked a bit like a giant prehistoric bird and would stalk menacingly about on stage effectively enough.

The "walking engines" had to look fearsome, technically accurate and historically appropriate. With their usual thoroughness, the Deans also took into account the reason the Martians were using them: not just to overrun humanity, but also to protect themselves. Wells describes them as clumsy, slimy octopi, soft-bodied and heavy, "the most sluggish things I ever saw crawl." Because they have only tentacles they need long mechanical legs and arms, and armour casing to move around in the increased pressure and poisonous atmosphere of an alien environment. In short, the machines were spacesuits, or, in Victorian terms, deep-sea diving suits.

It was crucial for both designers and artists not to be tempted to modernise Wells's original. Writing halfway between the Crimean War and World War One, he saw clearly that any future conflict would involve great machines of destruction. Martyn's research showed that "what the thinkers of the Victorian Age feared was the coming of the cast-iron cavalry." It was the appearance of nineteenth-century mechanical technology that he and Roger captured in their complexly articulated tripods. These were Victorian Martians, after all.

All the pictures you see here are illustrations for Wells's book. The original designs and a number of other paintings that work quite independently now form the nucleus of a wholly new project. Roger took them into discussions with Paramount Pictures, with SF model expert Martin Bower, and with other filmmakers and screenwriters. Consultations continue on a film development of the material—not another screen version of *The War of the Worlds*, but something intriguingly different.

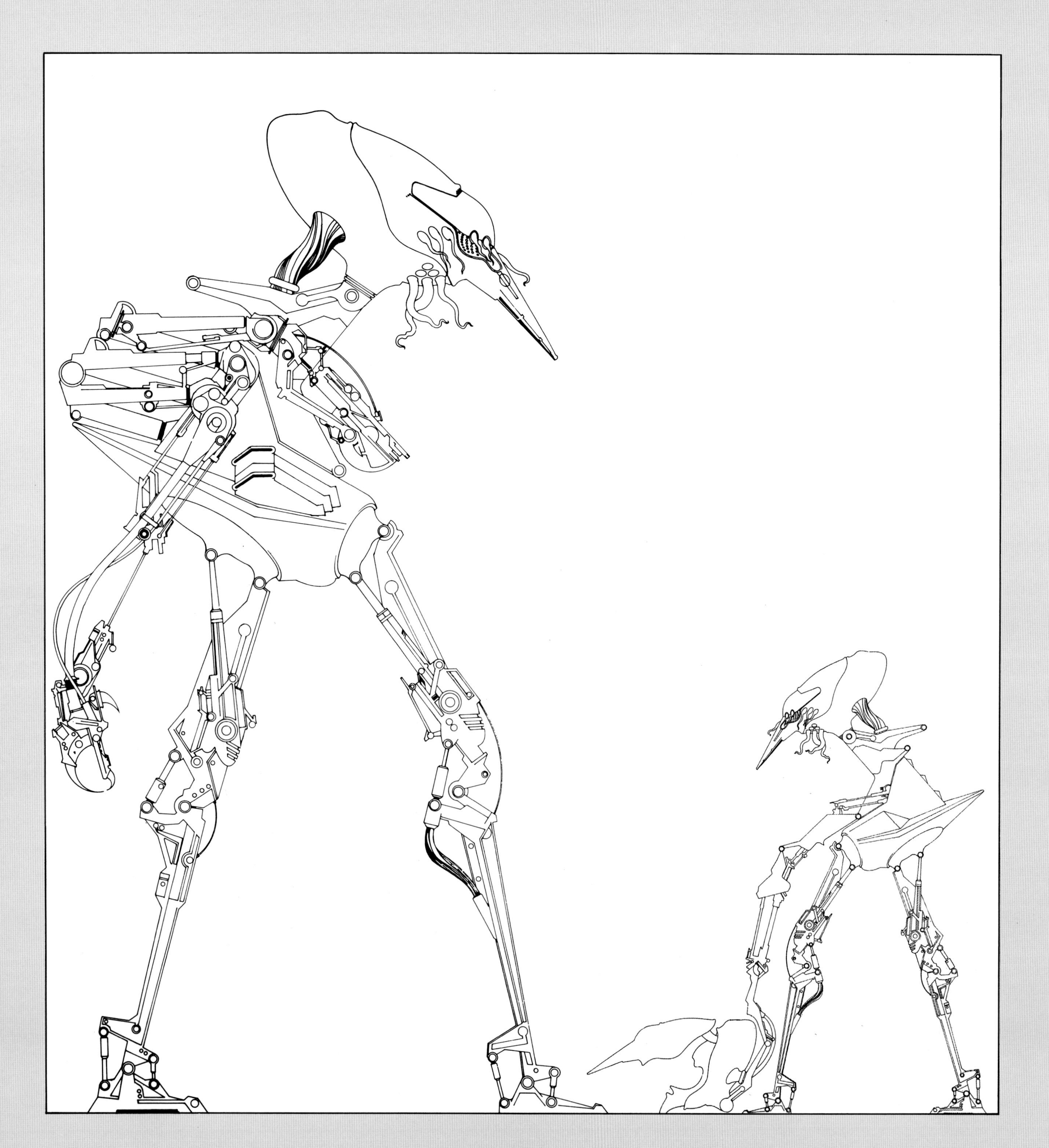

VIDEO PODS & GAMES

BARRY DEVLIN
BREAKING
STAR
CODES

Starcodes is a celebration of the twelve signs of the zodiac. The project was Barry Devlin's, founding member of the Irish rock band Horslips. In 1982 he asked Magnetic Storm to contribute to a series of video programmes incorporating music and dance. Their first involvement was to produce a painting for the album cover and a promotional brochure. Later would come graphics, pictures, backgrounds, sets and props. Roger started work on Pisces with two pictures of the same rock formation, by day and by night.

He followed his own fascination with landscape as sculpture in all the *Starcodes* paintings. Natural shapes were what was needed: architecture, even in the radical Tectonic style, would limit the historical scope, while the active figures he often puts into paintings to add a dimension of narrative time (see p. 83) would on this occasion be provided by the dancers themselves. The Pisces rock, appropriately for the sign of the fish, was based on the shape of a kind of coral, built up in stacks of platelets. Roger arrived at it by way of a design he was working on for a seaside pier supporting a roller coaster (see p. 160).

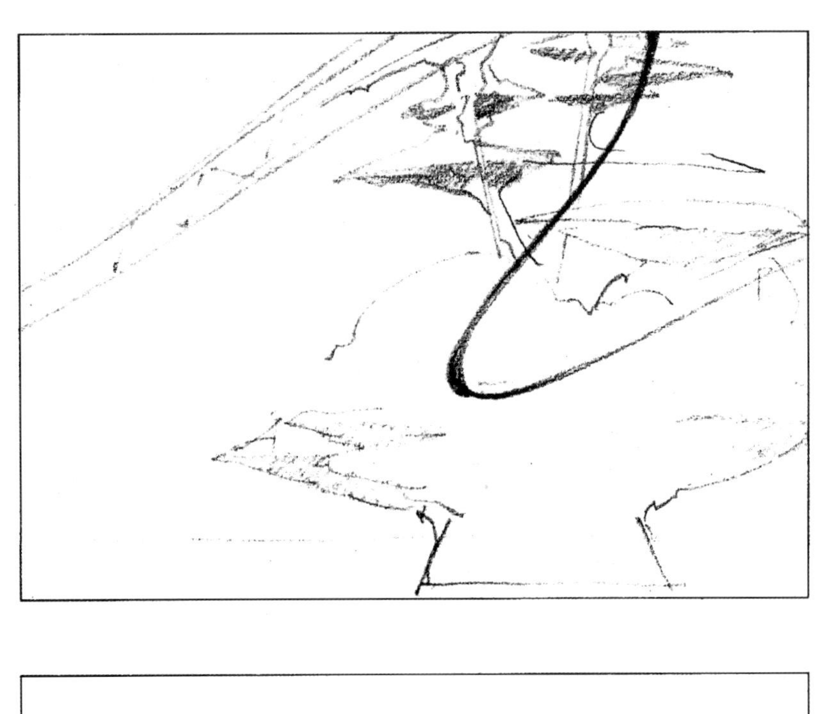
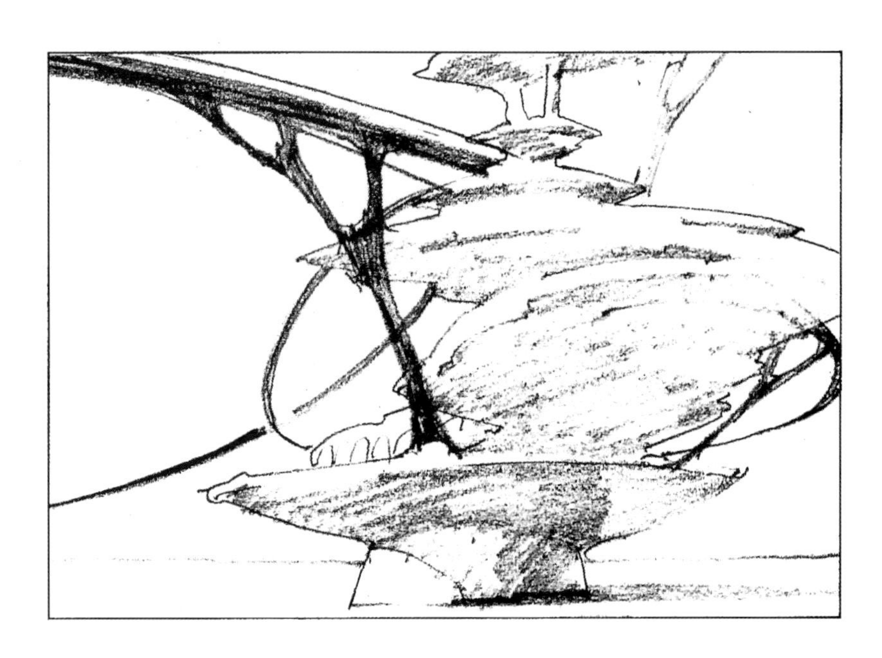

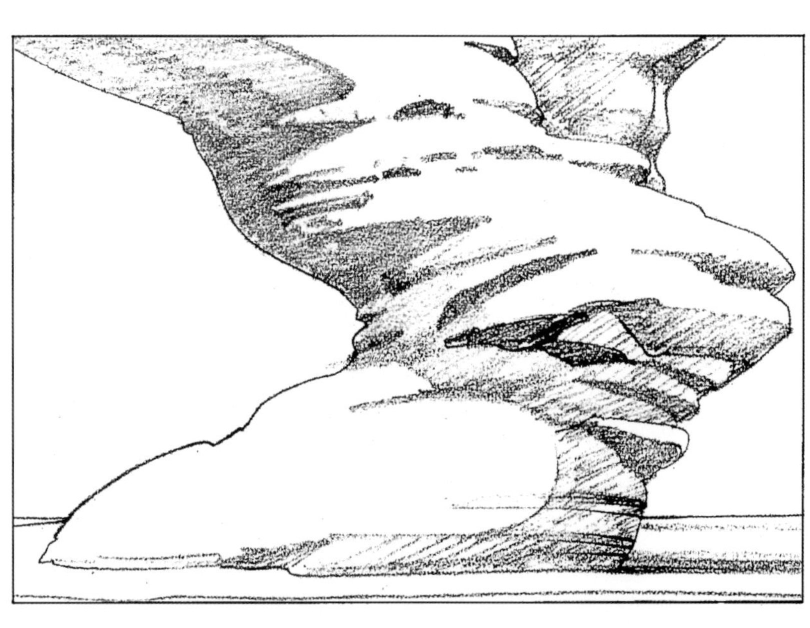

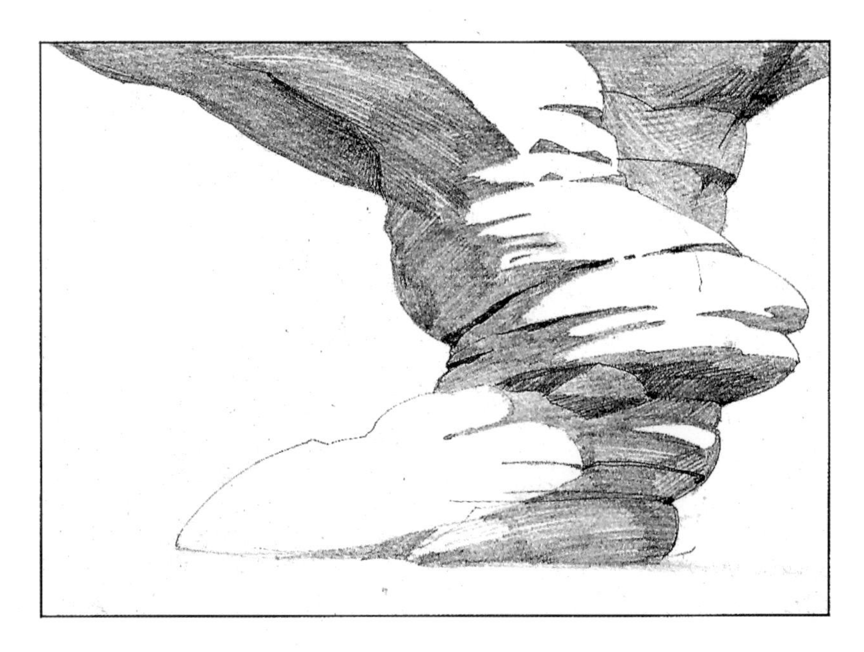

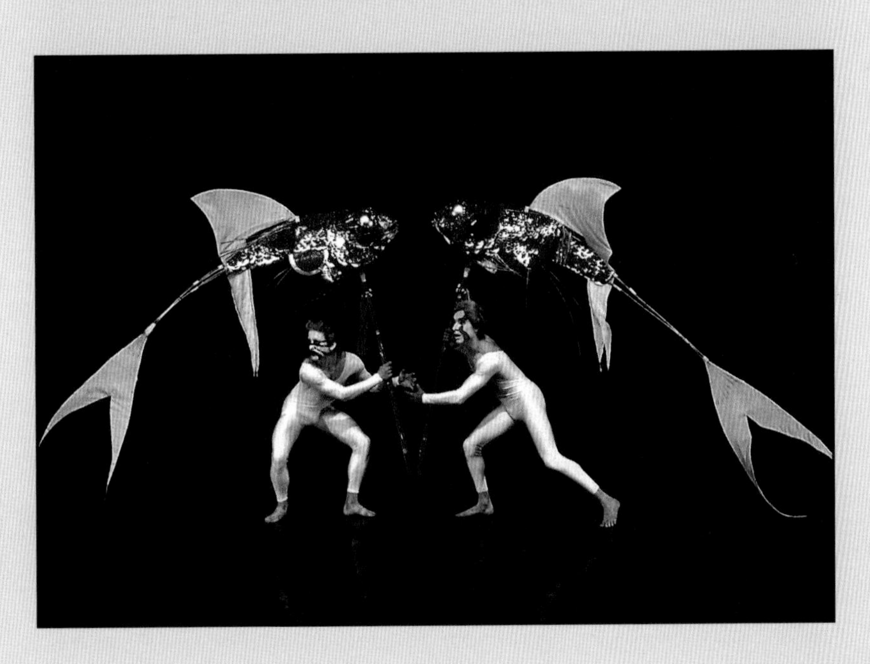

Around the rock fish swam in midair. The fish were totems on poles, made by Ian Miller, artist of *Green Dog Trumpet* and *Secret Art* (see p. 30). The video technique known as chromakey masked out the blue-cloaked dancers who operated the fish in the daylight sequence. At night, the fish appeared on their poles "like the war pennants of some Gothic army." The dancers, visibly superimposed this time, stole up, seized the fish and fled.

Barry Devlin wrote the twelve songs and performed them with his Starcodes band. The programmes were made in Radio Telefis Eireann studios, directed by Ian McGarry and designed by Alan Pleass with Ray Ball. With their help and encouragement, Roger and Martyn were able to extend the Magnetic Storm contribution considerably, developing it to best effect. The choreography was by Babil, of the Irish National Ballet, with additional material by Roger Dean. "I don't know anything about dance, much less choreography, but I did know what was required for dramatic tension. These people were creeping in to steal the war pennants. As they got hold of them there was a sense of added danger, then triumph: as they ran off with them, they were elated. Those were easily identifiable emotions, so, without interfering at all with the dance, I was able to say what was needed in terms of mime."

For Aries Barry had composed a song with a chorus reminiscent of a Gregorian chant. Roger's background was a huge interior, a sort of cathedral-cave. The camera zoomed in on a painting of a monk and then faded to a section of the cave wall, where three dancers appeared dressed as monks. This section of scenery was painted on the spot during a recording session.

Painting at this unaccustomed speed was a challenge, but a welcome one. Like many other artists' sketches, Roger's have a vigour that painting tends to disguise. Now he could attempt to capture in paint the vibrancy and rhythm of his most successful pencil work.

Magnetic Storm's work on camouflage (see p. 14) had prompted an investigation of the function of surface decoration. Natural markings, whether camouflage or display, reveal as much of an animal's character as its form. "Devising the Pisces and Leo makeup gave us the chance to try our conclusions out on real people, who had to sit still and be painted.

The symmetrical pattern on the back of the female cat-dancer proved difficult until the studio makeup artists cut a stencil. The male cat, energetically danced by Babil, wore a mask which was removed halfway through, showing make-up underneath.

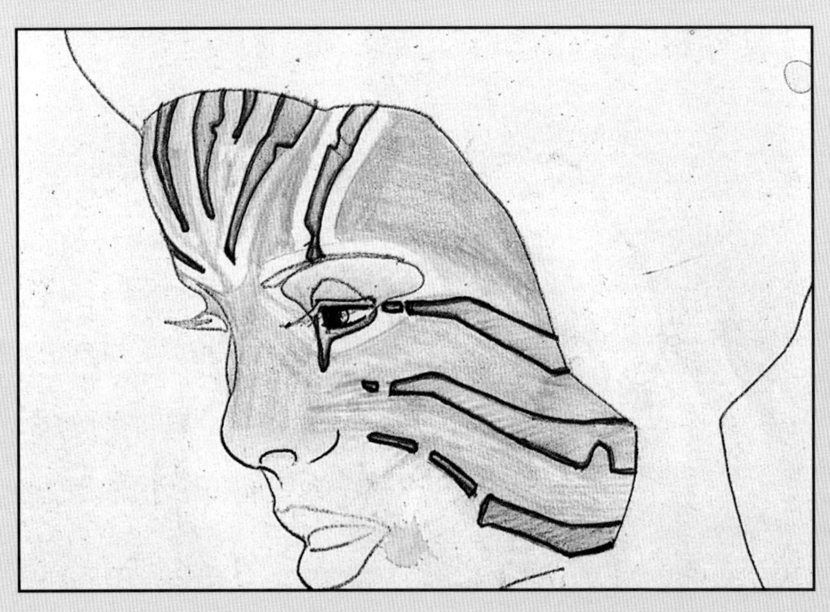
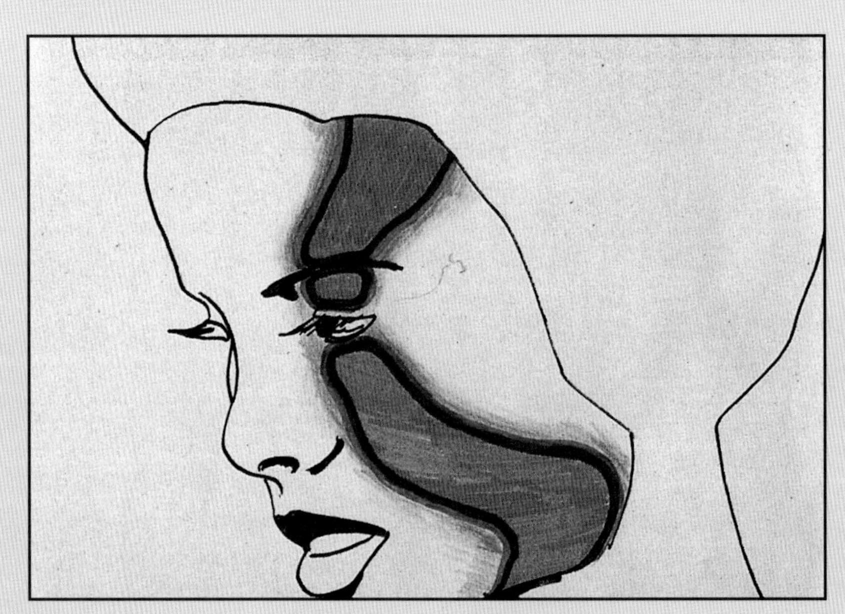

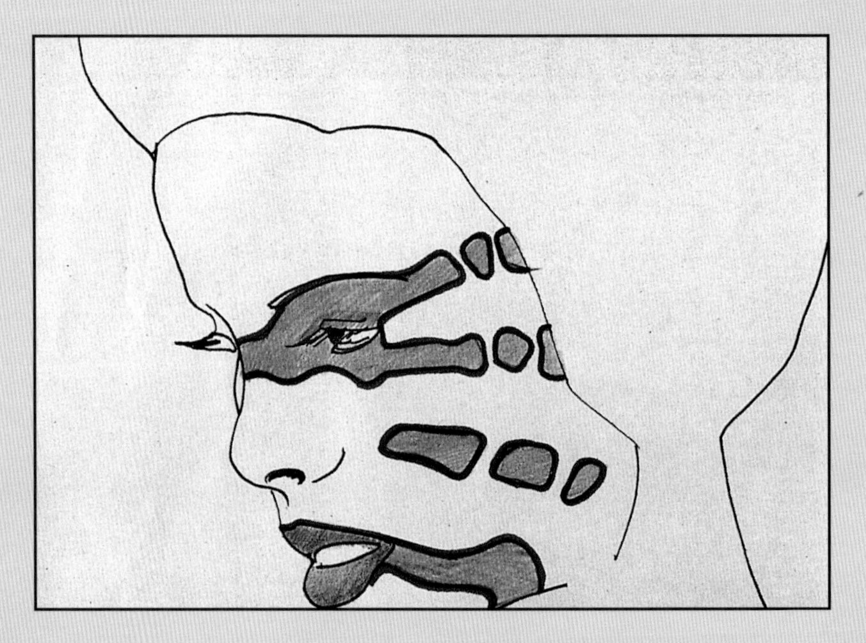

The decision to have two dancers for Leo instead of one was made quite late. Television performance often necessitates swift changes and rapid responses, not least because so many people are involved. The Leo head, like the Pisces fish, was by Ian Miller. For Aries Martyn commissioned the dancing monks' rams' heads and glowing eyes from Jeff Kazimir. The masks worn in Virgo were strongly influenced by the traditional characters of Venetian carnival and commedia dell'arte, with an added demon's head on a pole, sculpted by Billy Nicholas.

Martyn, with his background in film and stage work, was on familiar ground, but *Starcodes* gave Roger new experience in broadening his usual fields of design: from the zodiac glyphs to scripts and storyboards. It provided extended exposure to the conditions of film and television production, which Magnetic Storm is going on to develop.

Now when Hollywood calls on Magnetic Storm, the Dean brothers will more often say, "Yes, we're interested," where they used to say no, to cartoon films for instance, or pass the enquiry on to others. Projects currently in planning under negotiation include concept design and set construction for several other people's movies. "They're not our own projects, but the experience is immensely useful," says Roger. "It's a world we're just starting to work in, and there are still plenty of things to learn."

In that world, as in other areas of artistic enterprise, far more ideas are discussed than ever materialise. Magnetic Storm are considering twice as many invitations from film and television producers as original projects of their own—about the right proportion, Roger reckons. "Back in 1973 we had about ten book projects, including *Views* and *The Album Cover Album*. The other eight included some ideas that might one day be the best books we'd ever done; but we didn't follow them up then because they weren't the right *sort* of publishing for Paper Tiger or Dragon's Dream. By 1980 we were achieving perhaps six out of every ten new ideas that came along: at that level, an extraordinarily high success rate.

"Today, with film and television work, we're starting all over again with the ten projects of which two or three will reach the screen. Now we know how that pattern works: you cast your net wide at first, and then you draw it in. We're making a lot of new contacts, finding our way around the film world just as we had to in publishing. But this time we can do it with greater confidence. This time we don't have to make it up as we go along."

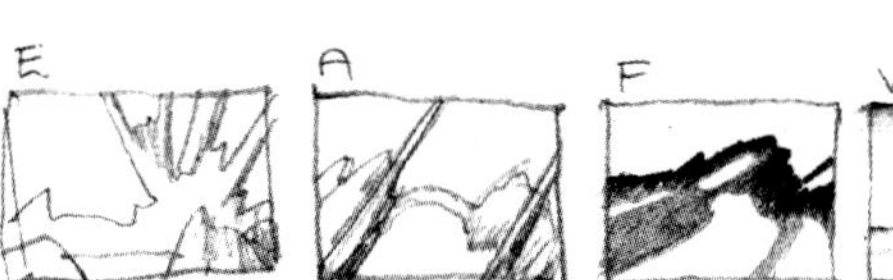
E
A
F
W

Roger's individual star-sign landscapes, and the four continuity paintings representing the four elements (earth, air, fire and water), were atmospheric interpretations. A bold, emphatic style was appropriate for television transmission, so he devised a loose, immediate technique. The finished paintings remain backdrops, not complete pictures in their own right, but they represent an important step in the advance of his painting skills.

ARCHITECTURE

ARCHITECTURE

More than sixty years later we still live in the shadow of the Bauhaus. Every day millions of people wake up in homes like migrant labour hostels, send their children to prefabricated aircraft hangars called schools, and work in the great Glass Box that stares down on every city street with cold, unblinking eyes. We live in the age of the Box, bequeathed to us by Walter Gropius, founder of the Bauhaus School, and his fellow Functionalists in Germany, Holland and France during the twenties and thirties.

In the wasteland of post-World War One Europe they dreamed of an absolutely pure architecture, a naked, clean, linear, functional, anti-bourgeois architecture for the proletariat; and with the fervour of religious converts they created a new wasteland of sterile uniformity. The Word spread to America and thence to England, where the building boom of the fifties and sixties saw the rise of box after concrete-and-steel box, relentlessly rectangular, charmless, like a factory if the client was lucky, like a public lavatory if he wasn't (but either way he had to put up *and* shut up—the architect was God).

It was heresy to permit anything to sully the pure vision. No curves, colours, follies, ornament or passion. Decoration was taboo, "useless embellishment." Privacy was bourgeois: every house and office had to be open plan, cosy as Siberia. For the purpose of design, buildings were regarded as containers for things, human or otherwise. The French Functionalist Le Corbusier called his houses "machines for living." Too bad that the good folk reacted by decking them out with chintzy patterned fabrics and pastel shades—anything to make those cold cells a home. Re-education was the cry.

This was architecture for the architects, the era of the award-winning slum. Scarcely had the architect received the critics' laurels for another Lubyanka tower block than the horny-handed sons of toil were scrawling obscenities in the corridors or hurling themselves off the fifteenth floor.

Yet such was—and still is—the received wisdom taught throughout the United States and Europe when Roger Dean entered the Royal College of Art in 1965. There he was fortunate to encounter a rare spirit of enlightenment. Encouraged to pursue his own path, he made every student's journey in search of first principles and returned with a blueprint for apostasy that would have given Herr Gropius gargoyles. It is not so uncommon now to hear voices of dissent crying in the wilderness, but twenty years ago the silence of consensus was virtually unbroken.

The basis of Functionalist theory is the formula "form follows function." In other words, the mechanical function an object is said to perform must define its basic struc-ture. It is also decreed that the designer must adhere strictly to the utilitarian process of manufacture (e.g., one S-bend of steel tubing makes a chair, not two) and the sanctity of the material used (e.g., wood must not be painted).

Roger Dean recognised that Functionalism was inadequate precisely because it saw everything in mechanical terms. It simply did not have the means to understand the essential nature of an object or building—what, pray, can the mechanics of a crucifix tell you about its essence? And because of that failure of understanding it was incapable of perceiving an object's true function. This led to the definition of a house as a "machine for living." Roger, however, defined the essence of a home as a place that provided security and privacy. He saw man as essentially an animal, with the same primordial fears of vulnerability and territorial disadvantage, dark corners and hidden spaces. To feel "at home" a person had to feel secure.

To complete his apostasy he rejected the Functionalist view of surface markings as mere decoration. In nature, markings are the very basis of survival. They are part of the essence of an animal: a tiger without stripes is not a tiger.

Roger uses surface markings in the same way, to emphasise the essence of a building. The choice of style is almost unlimited. To take a lighthearted example, on the Greenslade record cover he added decorative black beams to the demon's castle to create the illusion of a mock Tudor cottage, which would not look out of place (though its occupier might) in a Surrey suburb.

He began by studying archetypal architecture—caves, boats and tree houses—and what makes them attractive to be in. All, in different ways, promote a palpable feeling of security. A cave provides absolute control over access, preventing a predator on the outside from determining whether it is a small alcove or a gigantic labyrinth. He enters blind and is seen long before he sees his prey. A boat is intrinsically vulnerable, but its particular attraction is the immediate contrast between its cosy security and the primeval elements raging outside. A tree house has the advantage of height—frightened animals run up trees for safety—but to be totally secure it should ideally be situated on a hilltop in a wood, giving a clear view down and around but being itself concealed. Visual advantage is crucial. In keeping with the animal metaphor Roger Dean designed a tree house (see p. 142) like a cluster of bird's nests.

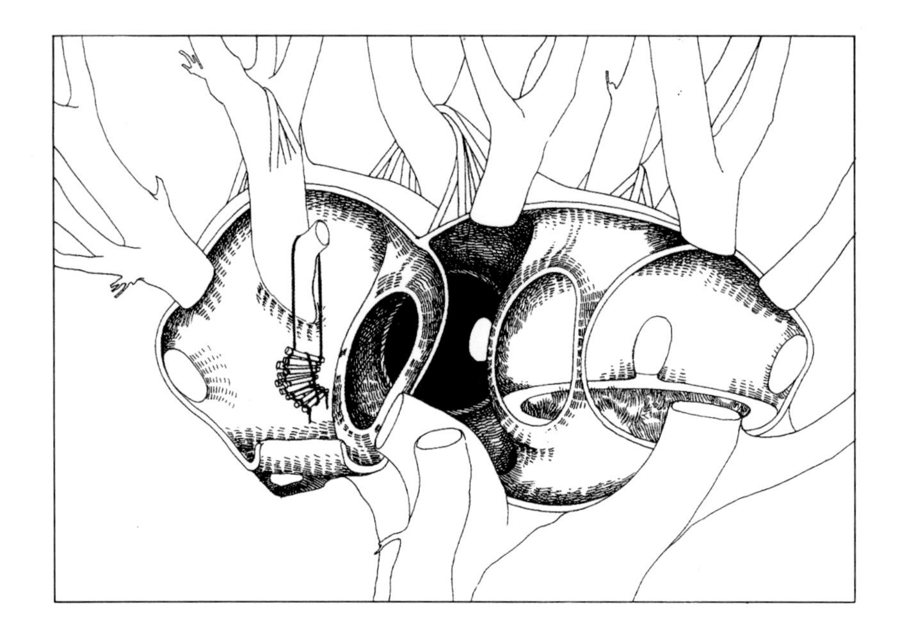

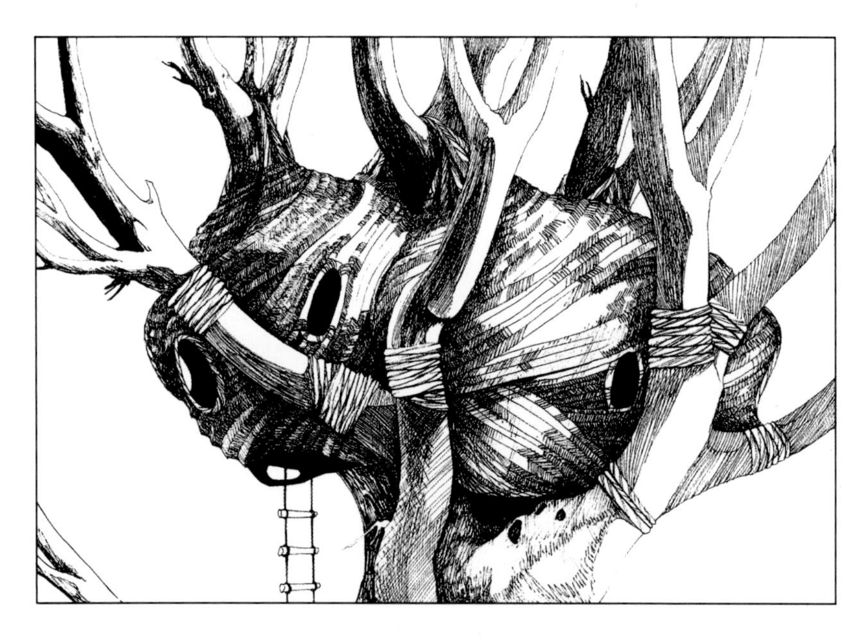

The key to his buildings is "strategic control of space". In effect, he created a martial art of domestic architecture. Of course, people in civilised societies do not live, as animals do, in constant fear of attack. But there is abundant everyday evidence that they are more at ease in a place where they feel instinctively secure, regardless of whether there is any actual threat. This has nothing to do with the crime statistics; it is an instinctive response to surroundings. Take, for example, the way people react when entering a restaurant. They seem irresistibly drawn to a corner where they can sit with their backs to the wall. What they are doing, albeit subconsciously, is avoiding the possibility of movement at the back of their necks—every animal's weak spot. Daily life provides copious illustration of the unease and irritation that people feel when someone is lurking behind them.

Archetypal architecture was both the starting point for and the extreme example of Roger Dean's instinctive theory. From there he moved on to a study of children's bedrooms (see *Views* pp. 134–144). Children know instinctively whether a room or building feels right. In adults that instinct is blurred by the sophistication of taste. But, as Roger discovered, it is possible to design a bedroom in which no one, adult or child, could spend a restful night, or one that gives the best chance of a good sleep. Comfort in sleep has more to do with the "feel" of the room than of the bed.

The children he interviewed all listed the same likes and dislikes about bedrooms. They were made uneasy by hidden spaces—under the bed, behind curtains and cupboard doors—and by the spooky outline of hanging clothes. They wanted, above all, a clear view of the door from the bed and, when tucked in, to be at eye level with a standing adult. The answer was a "cave in the wall" bed, into which the child had to climb. The curved walls, an arm's length in diameter, gave the snug feeling of a favourite hiding place without a trace of claustrophobia.

From this radical (in its essential sense of "from the roots") approach Roger Dean conceived a basic architectural form—a round, womb-like room that, arranged in clusters, grew to form houses, flats, hotels, office towers and multimillion-pound entertainment centres.

The new shapes required new building techniques; clearly bricks and mortar were no use. He devised a method of using sprayed concrete, called gunnite, on fibreglass moulds. This had the added advantage of being substantially faster and cheaper than conventional techniques. "If Sydney Opera House had been built in gunnite, it would have cost a tenth and been built in a hundredth of the time," he says.

A different kind of architectural drawing was also called for. The standard plan and elevation could not convey all that had to be said about the shape of these buildings. Computer

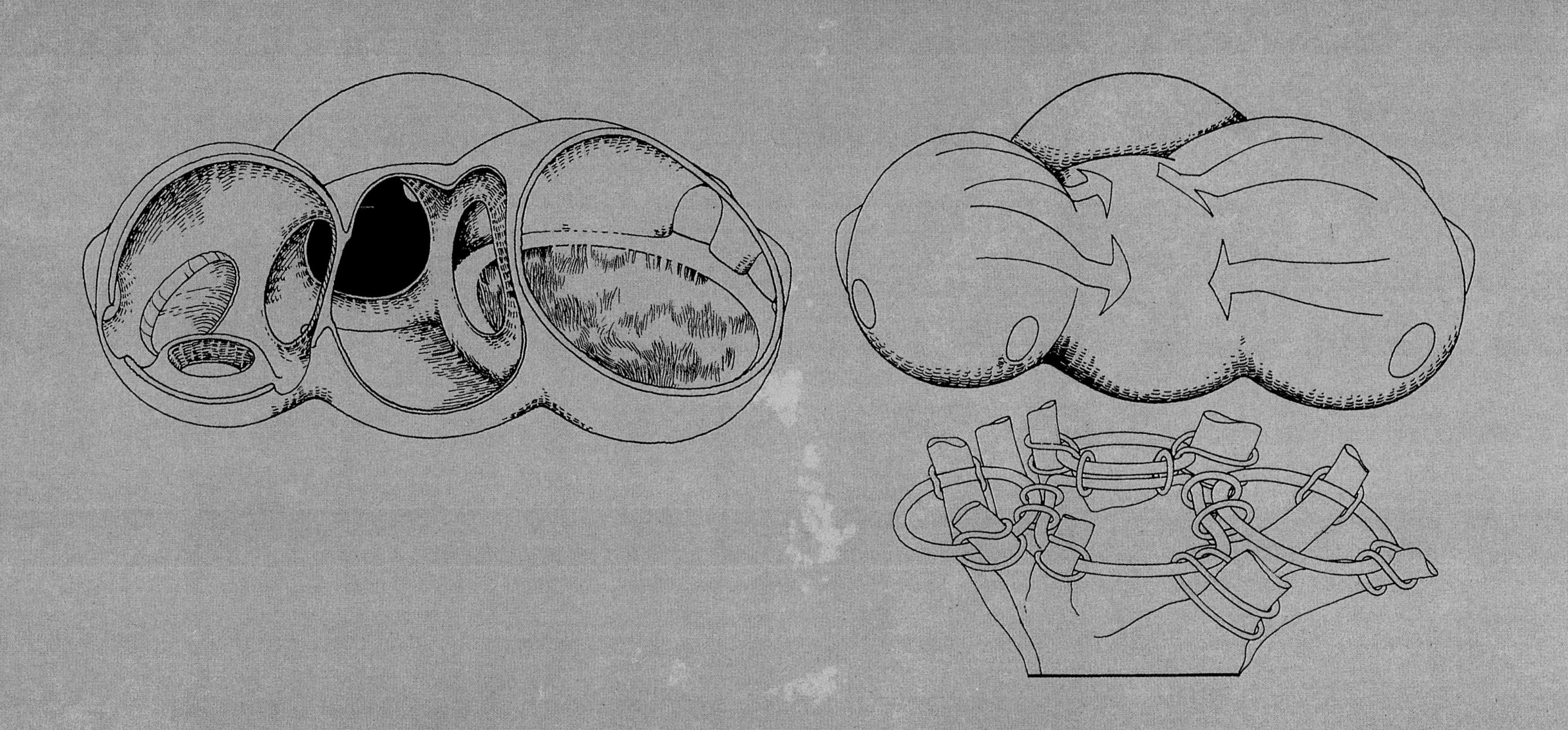

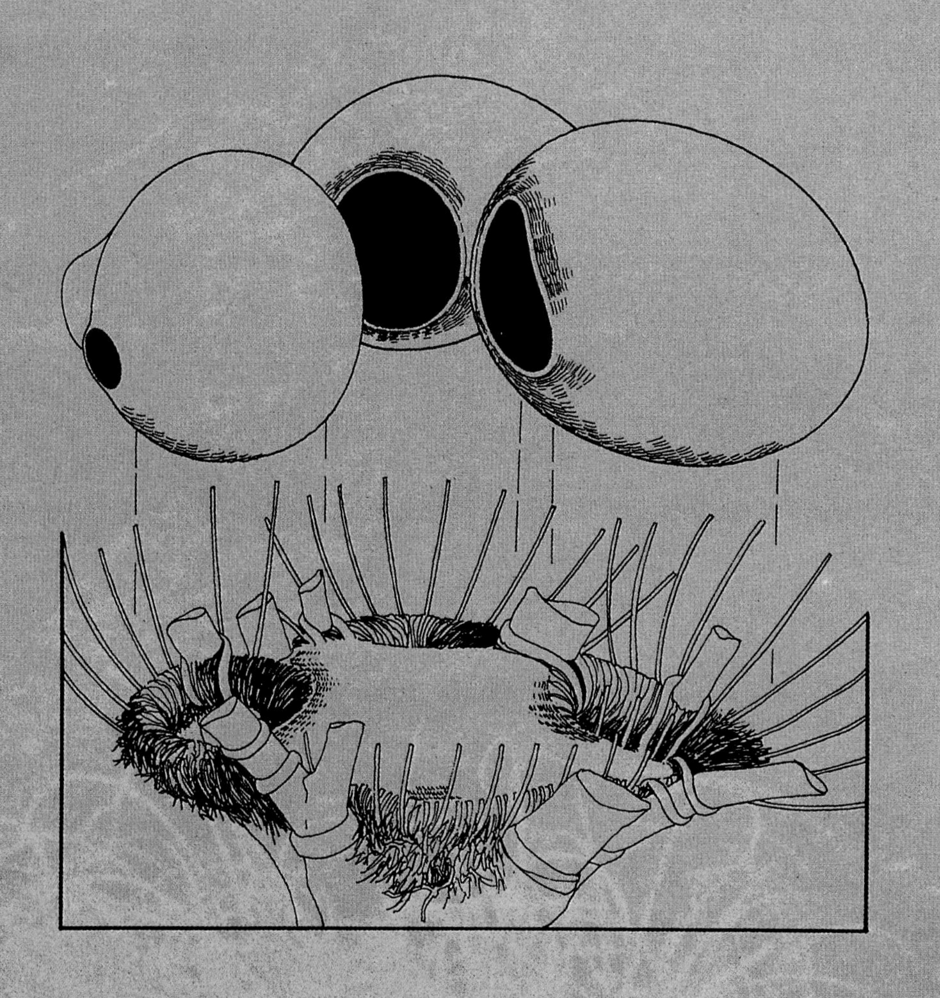

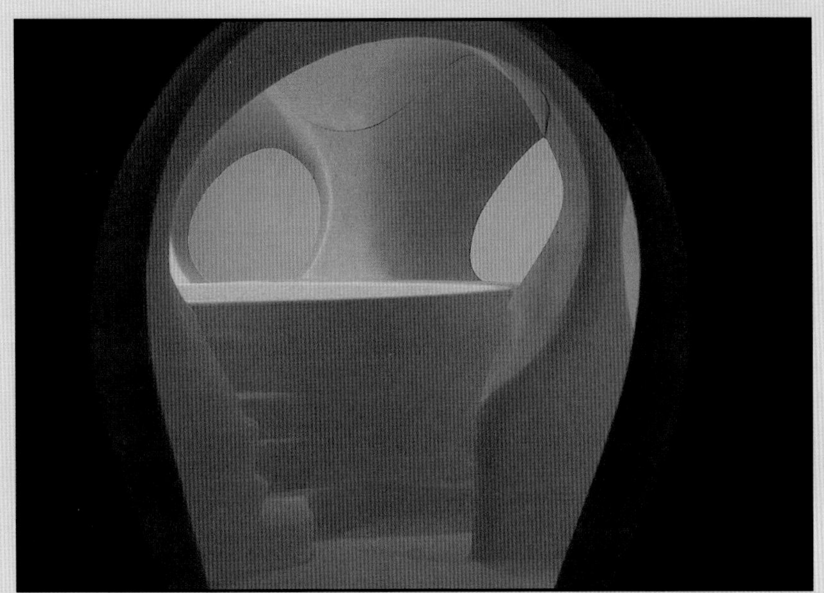

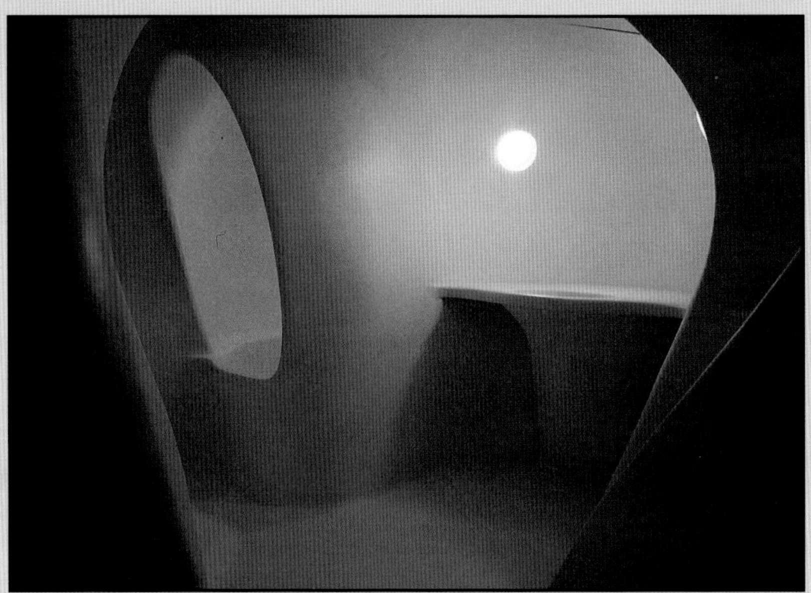

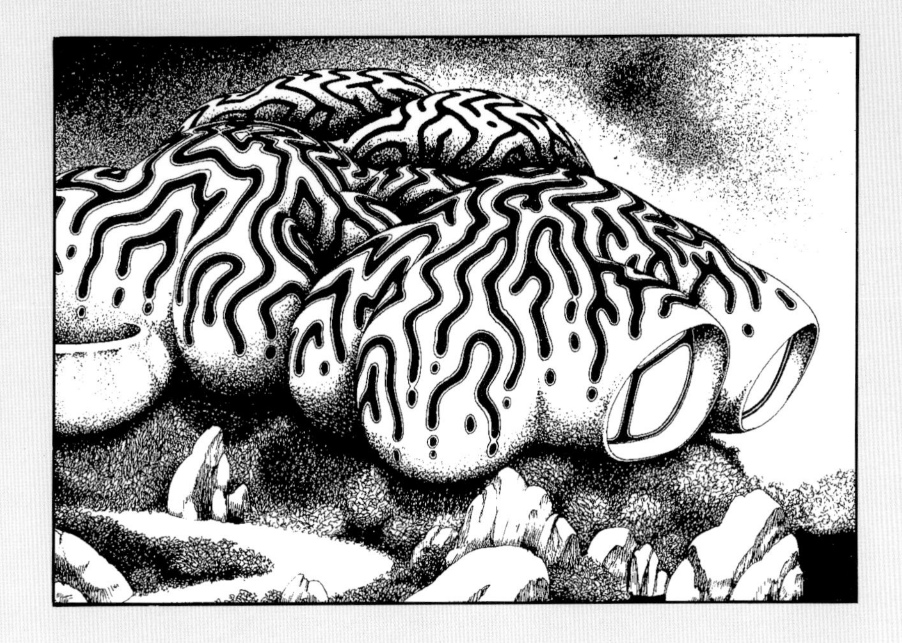

programs would be used in the design process, but to give an impression of what the structures looked like he reached for his paint and brushes. The paintings became a phenomenon in their own right, selling thirty million copies worldwide as posters, cards and record covers, and, incidentally, recruiting enthusiastic popular support for the architecture.

For all their exotic appearance those tulip-topped towers and puff-ball villages were serious building projects. Engineers had confirmed the strength of the structures and the astounding efficiency of gunnite. Yet the building *looked* so improbable. The Deans' problem was how to introduce people to a domestic architecture unlike anything they had ever seen. Something as permanent as a house was not a good first step. What about a holiday cottage or hotel? A short stay would give people the chance to try out the shapes "on approval" and lose their aesthetic inhibitions. There was also the initial cost of a prototype, which made a 300-room hotel the minimum feasible size.

Fate intervened in the unlikely shape of the Seacon science fiction exhibition in Brighton in August 1979. As a final fling in their publishing business, the Dean brothers were staging a display of book covers, paintings and backdrops. There were people wandering around in Darth Vader outfits and wide-eyed SF fantasy fanatics muttering "Beam me up, Scotty." Amid this quaint lunacy, representatives of a group working with the company For Sport By Sport approached the brothers and asked them to design a mini theme park as an adjunct to a sports centre. Planning objections killed the scheme before the Deans had started work, but fruitful contacts had been made, soon to be renewed during the curious saga of the Brighton Marina development.

An important lesson had also been learnt: Magnetic Storm, consisting of Roger and Martyn Dean and Rob Fitzgerald, was far too small a base from which to carry through a major building project. They had the design skills in abundance but lacked the practical experience and specialist staff. New Era Tectonic Developments Ltd. was formed to fill the gap. John Packer, a partner in W. F. Johnson and Partners, an architectural and engineering firm, brought in his specialist staff. Diane Courtney and Brian Eagles, partners in the London law firm Herbert Oppenheimer, Nathan and Van Dyk kept a legal eye on development and promotion of projects; and Graham Skelcy of Montague Evans, the quantity surveyors, provided the planning expertise. Together with the Deans and Rob Fitzgerald, a former banker who acted as company secretary, they made up the NETD team.

It so happened that just at this time an interview with Roger Dean about his architecture was shown on Southern Television. Two Brighton councillors who saw it were struck by one particular remark he made: "You could build a house in a rubbish pit. You simply create the landscape around it." He has always believed that the criterion of human response applies as much to landscaping as to building. Landscapes have to be choreographed to entertain, surprise, amaze, and provide a fitting contrast to the buildings that inhabit it.

In the plans for the 500-bed Marina hotel that he was asked to submit to the Brighton Marina board, Roger designed two and a half miles of corridor, which wind their serpentine way through and around the building—a walkway full of events and panoramas, follies and sudden alcoves bright with illuminated coral reefs of fibreglass. At the same time there are cross-paths making shortcuts to the lifts.

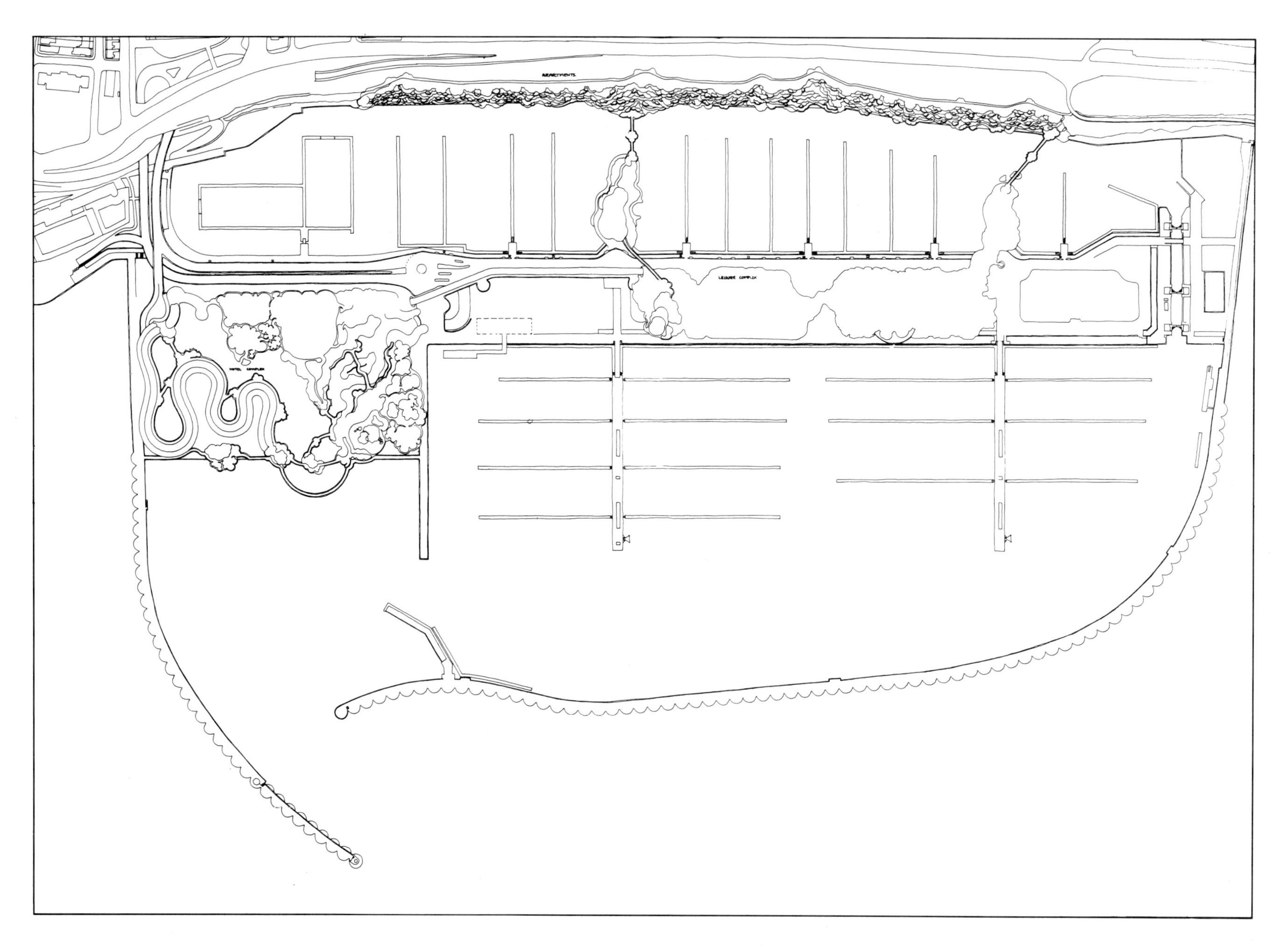
APARTMENTS
LEISURE COMPLEX
HOTEL COMPLEX

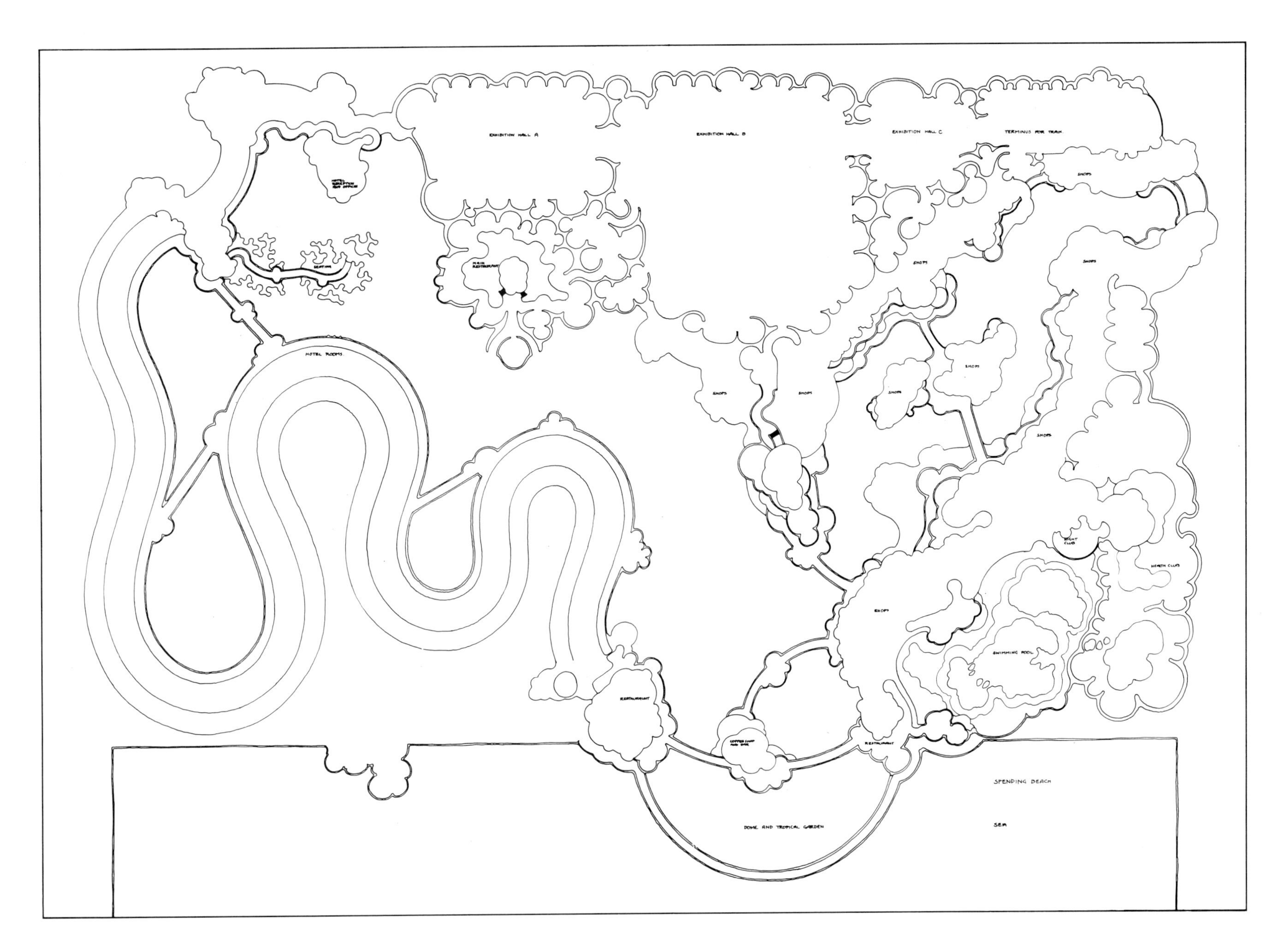

The whole project, which included 860 flats rising in terraces, with shops and a nursery school, entertainment and exhibition facilities, was to be completed in two phases costing £35 million each. The Dean brothers secured the backing of several building, electrical and leisure groups and, under intense pressure to be ready for a meeting of the Brighton Marina board in August 1980, began work on a feasibility study, drawings and a quarter-scale model of a suite for the hotel (see p. 144). They met the deadline. They handed in the finished portfolio. But it was never presented to the board. To this day no satisfactory explanation has been given. An inventive, thoughtful project was lost.

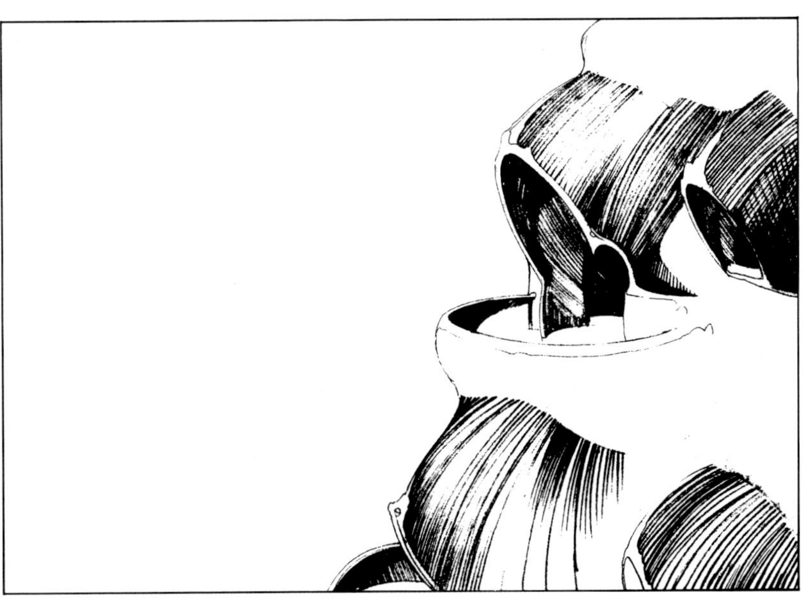

Public interest, however, was gaining momentum. Even as the road to Brighton pier petered out, a new, exciting avenue opened. It led up the M1 motorway to Birmingham and the International Ideal Home Exhibition, organised by Industrial and Trade Fairs at the National Exhibition Centre. One week after vainly meeting the Marina deadline, the Deans had been asked by John Talbot of ITF to provide a feature for the exhibition. They suggested that they build a full-size, fibre-glass prototype of the Marina hotel suite model. The idea was given the go-ahead in January 1981.

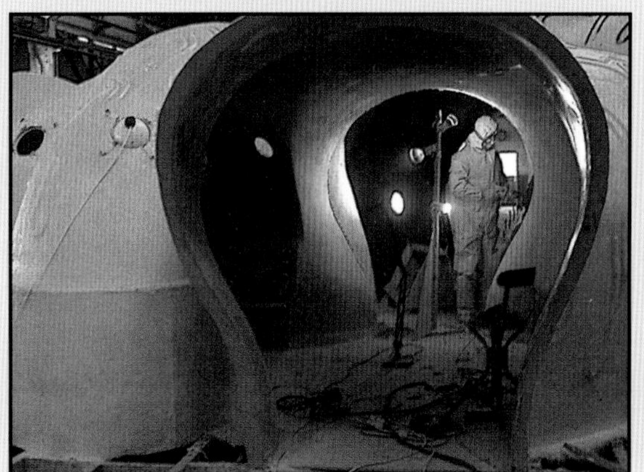

eck & Pollitzer
FOR
HIRE

Dewsbury & Pro

The hotel suite was built in a rented Brighton factory by a team led by four craftsmen: Bill Harling, sculptor and pattern-maker; Ian Harper, owner of the fibreglass company that helped build Martyn Dean's Drama stage for Yes; Tony Blackwell, master carpenter; and Peter Hall, wine grower, opera producer and, on this occasion, essential helper. They worked without drawings and with virtually no experience with the shapes. "Just follow the model," Roger blithely directed, leaving Martyn in charge of the operation. Amazingly, they completed the task in five weeks.

For an actual building, obviously gunnite is used instead of fibreglass. It is sprayed under extreme pressure onto moulds. A very dry mixture is used so that a ceiling can be sprayed without the gunnite running. It takes three days to "cure," but immediately after being sprayed it is solid enough to be carved like cheese to form unmoulded shapes, such as the top of a stairway. To make towers, each floor is sprayed in position in a steel superstructure. Any large spans between the moulded shapes are made by spraying gunnite onto a wire mesh. Being ovoid, the rooms are structurally very strong.

This method of construction is amazingly fast by conventional standards. A team of three could build a hotel suite in a day once full production was under way. In the Brighton Marina hotel, which has seventy rooms on each floor, a whole floor could be completed in only twelve days. Gunnite is also much cheaper, even taking into account the high cost of "tooling up" to make the first moulds—about a million pounds.

A bonus of gunnite is that it has incredible insulation properties. In addition, the curved walls keep warm air circulating because there are not top corners for it to become trapped in. As a result, the bedroom, say, can be kept at 20°C (68°F) with just two hundred watts, the equivalent of the body heat of two people.

The prototype hotel suite became the showpiece of the exhibition. Up to 20,000 people stood in line every day for nearly three weeks to peer, touch and exclaim their wonder. They came from every walk of life: young families and pensioners, jobless teenagers and rich Midlands businessmen.

The suite was built as a test experience, an introduction to this new concept of domestic architecture; it became an instrument of mass conversion. People seemed to fall under a spell the moment they entered. Instead of filing dutifully in one end and out of the other, they would not leave. They sat happily in the chairs marked "Keep off" and followed the children into the roped-off bedroom and clambered onto the bed, where they sprawled contentedly, swinging their legs and chatting. In short, they made themselves at home.

The complexity of this warren of rooms brought the excitement of adventure. Round every curve was something to explore, another brightly lit alcove drawing the eye and sharpening the curiosity. There seemed so many places to go. The raised bed and bath were rooms in themselves, adding to the illusion of space. People were heard to say on leaving: "We've missed the kitchen, let's go back"—even though there was no kitchen (this being a hotel suite). But it was easy to be mistaken; there *might* have been one tucked away off a turning in the labyrinth.

A businessman offered to pay cash for the suite on the spot, so that he could stick it on the end of his house "like a glowworm on a stone," as Roger Dean wryly commented. Then the letters started arriving. A young wife from Leicestershire with a five-year-old daughter and sons aged three and one wrote: "We have just seen your design for a futuristic house on 'ATV Today'. We think it's fantastic and feel it would be ideal for our accident-prone kids, with no corners to bump into." (Security, that basic principle in the theory, was to recur unprompted again and again.) The woman went on to suggest that her family should live in the suite for a trial period.

As this was a demonstration model, compromises had to be made in the design. In order to help the flow of visitors the suite is open ended and has no doors. In the bedroom there are modifications of the children's "cave in the wall" design, which is an extreme, archetypal structure, precisely meeting the criteria of security and privacy. The suite bedroom, aimed at adults, has a bed reached by walking up three steps rather than by climbing into an alcove. There is also space round the bed to give hotel staff and guests more room, and the bed is obviously less enclosed than in the children's "cave." But the instinctive principles of design can still be traced.

The light bulb shape of the rooms, although it makes a big impact, is essentially anonymous, an empty starting point receptive to a wide variety of decorative styles. Roger Dean looked for a craft-based style for the prototype, something people would recognise. Above all, he wanted to avoid the futuristic tag of SF gadgetry. In the bedroom the oriental style is defined simply and subtly by the blinds, which open out like Japanese fans. (The windows and blinds were made by David Evans, the upholstery and bedspread by Felicity Youette, and the glass was blown by Peter Layton.)

The exhibition gave the public its first taste of a Roger Dean building, and the response was overwhelming. A group of backers of the Brighton Marina project who went to see it were so impressed by the popular enthusiasm they were adamant that it should not be wasted. This led to the first tentative steps toward the proposed development of an ambitious theme park complex on land adjacent to the NEC. Surrounded by two motorways and the main Birmingham-to-Coventry road, it is, without exaggeration, one of the key development sites in Britain.

Roger Dean set out to design a complex that would astound, amaze and fill people with wonder. His aim was to create more than a Disneyland; it was to build a prototype of a city nucleus of the future—a vision of what the heart of Birmingham or Chicago or Sydney could look like.

The central attraction is a single structure, covered by a gigantic dome 300 metres across. This airy expanse contains tropical gardens, shops, plazas, cafes and restaurants, and the starting point for numerous rides. Some of the rides are high-speed, corkscrew roller coasters soaring high into the dome; others travel more sedately into a network of tunnels and coves filled with stunning simulations of space travel or artificial scenes such as a fibreglass coral garden lit from the inside with laser effects to re-create the wonder of the ocean bed. The rides lead out of the domed area through tunnels into underground warehouses like a vast film set, landscaped over with trees and hills so that only a few domes and glistening stalagmite towers are seen.

Elsewhere in the development are a hotel, shops, restaurants and a 1,000-home holiday village in a lake, like a fantastic Venice. Decorative ceramics and sculptures adorn balustrades, balconies and terraces, and bridges and pathways connect the islands. The whole area will be a visual attraction for day visitors to walk around.

Linked to both the accommodation and entertainment buildings is an activity area with a swimming pool; skating rinks; facilities for tennis, squash and keep-fit; and a nightclub and discos.

The visitor will enter literally a new world full of beauty and wonder.

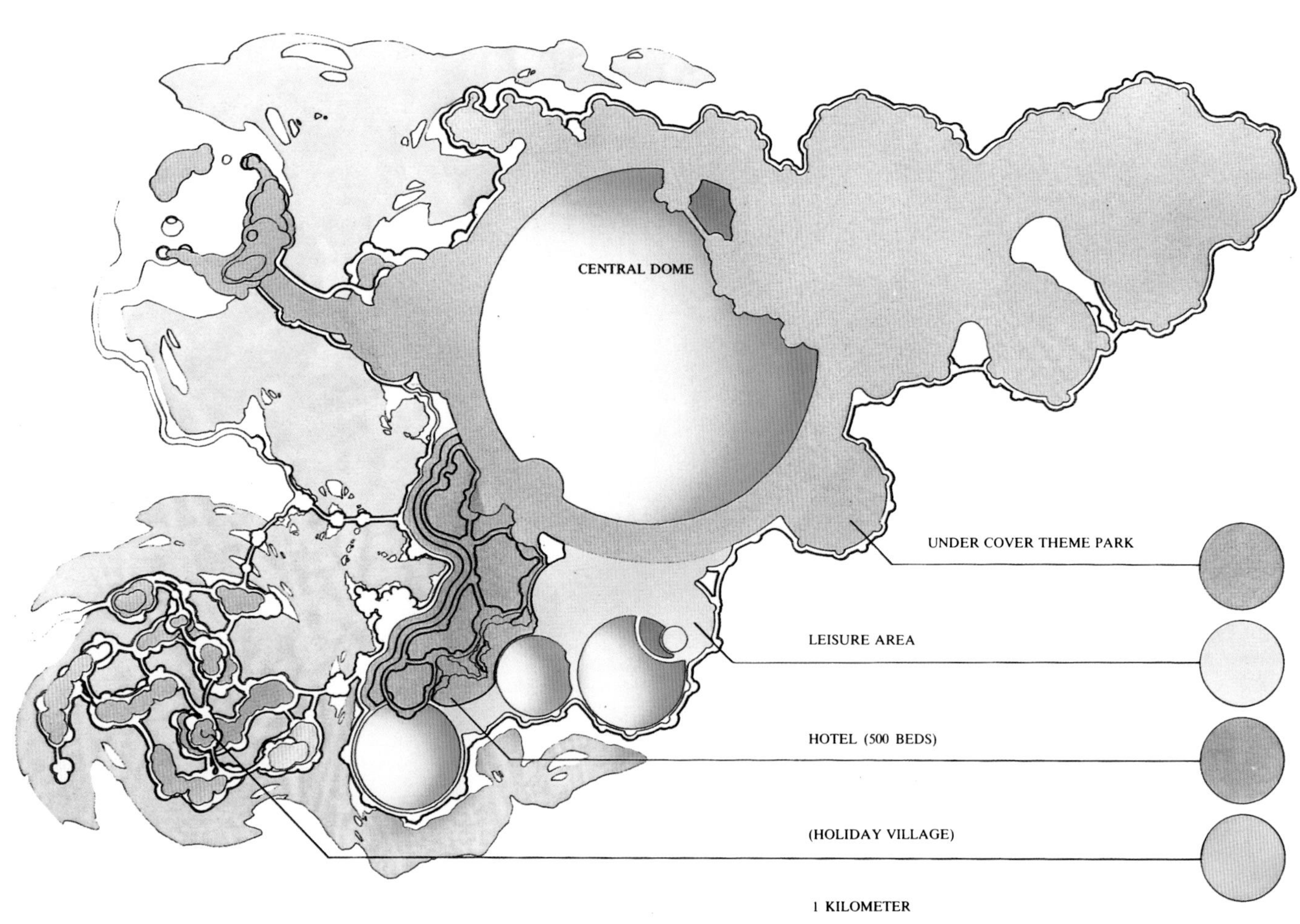
CENTRAL DOME
UNDER COVER THEME PARK
LEISURE AREA
HOTEL (500 BEDS)
(HOLIDAY VILLAGE)
1 KILOMETER

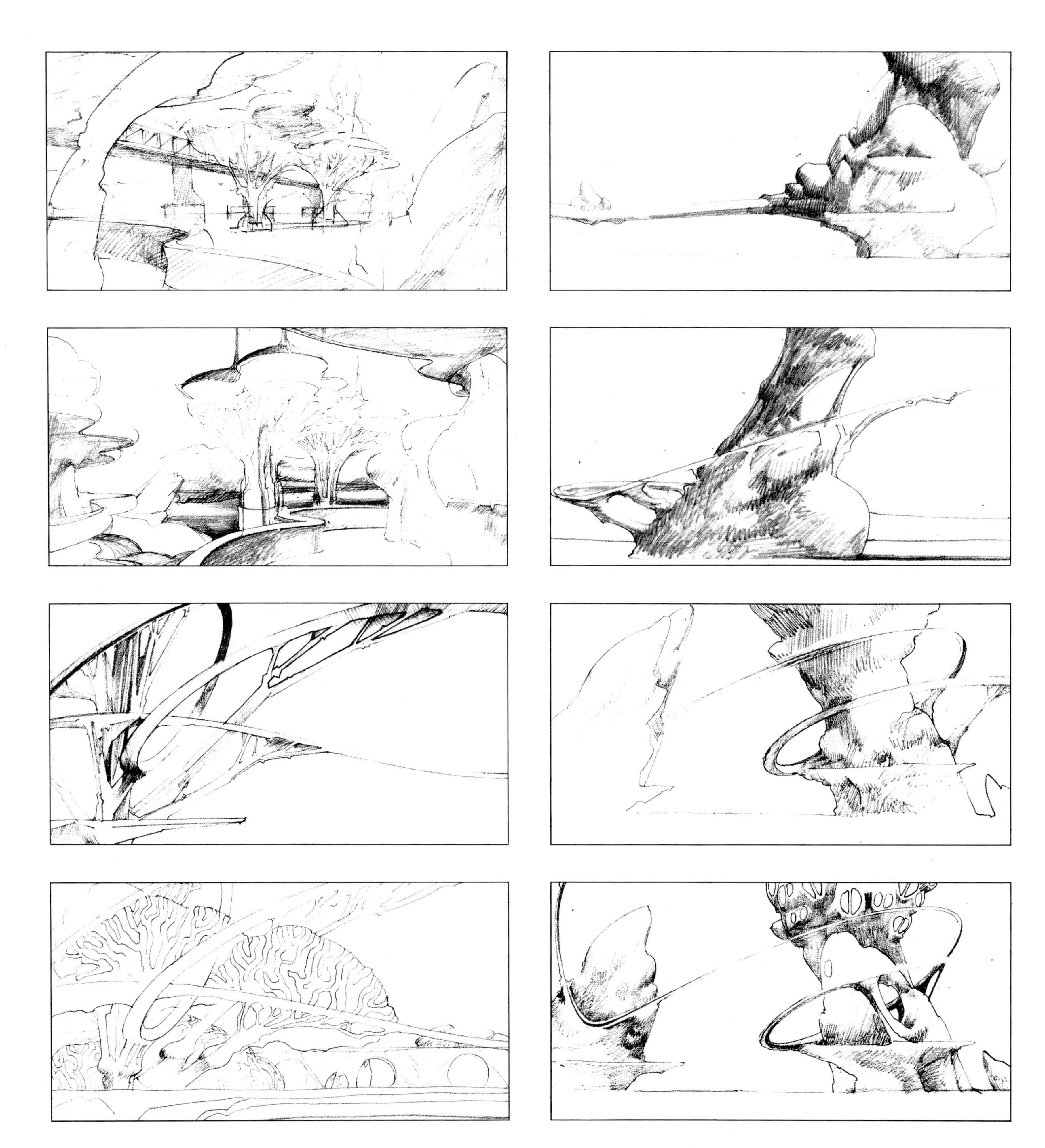

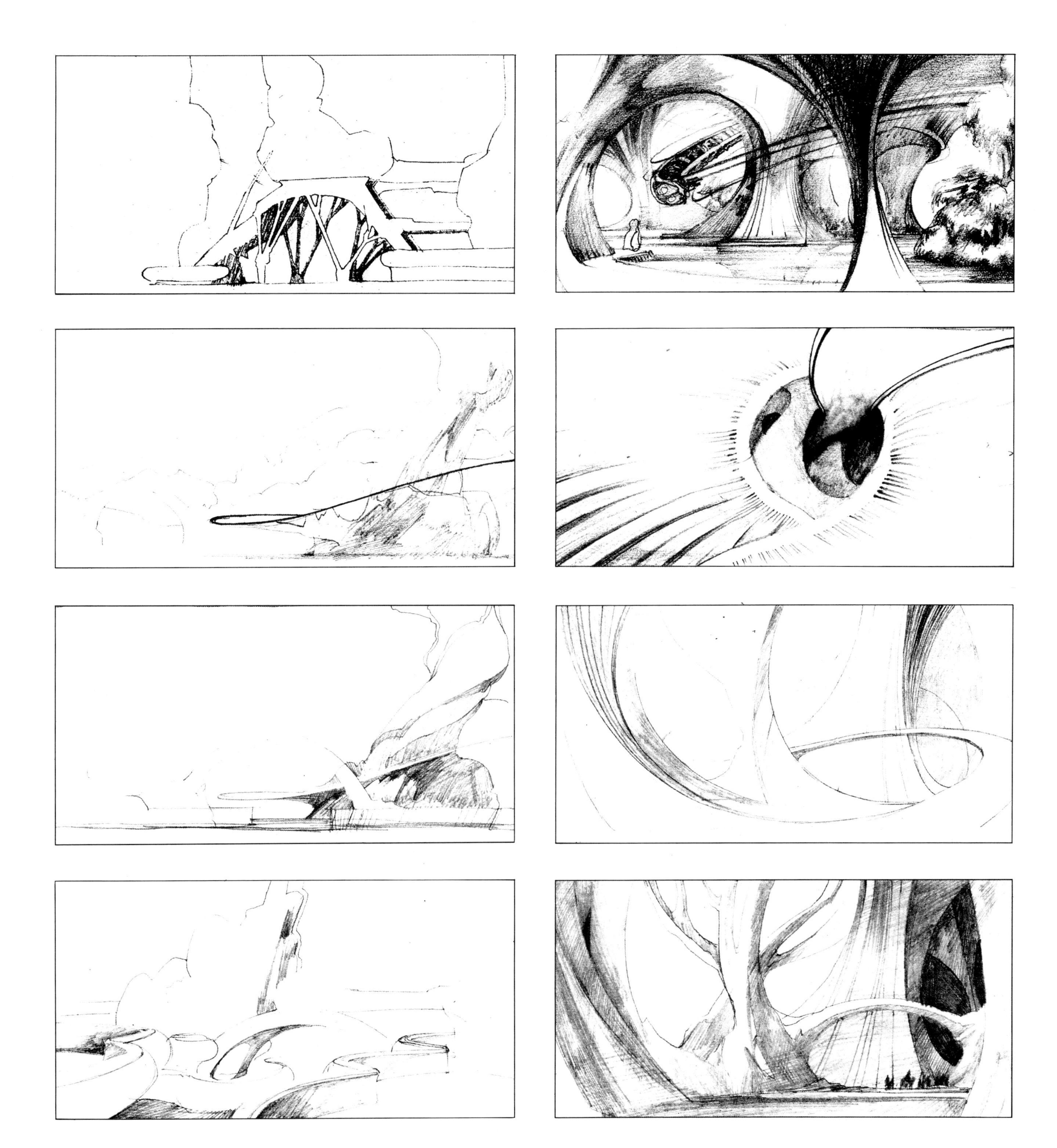

New projects began to pile up thick and fast in Magnetic Storm's portfolio, ranging from sport, entertainment and accommodation facilities at a site near London (June 1982) to a design contest for a park and property redevelopment in Paris (December 1982). Sketches and drawings were done, financial backing sought and the slow wheels of the planning process set in motion. The projects were all being promoted by NETD, but some had the benefit of a specific client.

In January 1983 the Deans were approached by an international consortium and asked to produce a sketch plan and colour paintings of a proposed cultural, leisure and property complex nearby Australia's most famous building—the Sydney Opera House—in one of the world's most beautiful harbours.

SUBUD DEVELOPMENT
DARLING HARBOUR
FOR SUSILA DHARMA PTY LTD
DESIGNED BY MAGNETIC STORM LTD / ROGER DEAN ©
SCALE
METRES

It is intended to be a glittering monument to Australia's bicentenary in 1988. Subud, the worldwide spiritual and charitable group behind the scheme, calls it "a green lung for Sydney." The incomparable site borders on the most expensive real estate in the city, taking in the docks and marshalling yards round Darling Harbour and the old wooden Pyrmont Bridge across the harbour itself. Straddling the bridge is the focal point of the proposed development, the International Pavilion. Roger Dean tackled this by designing the basic structure and then adding decorative "quotations" from architectural styles from around the world—minarets from Turkey, domes from the Kremlin and Bangkok—to highlight the international theme.

Across the harbour is the soaring, rocketship outline of the Green Cathedral, a glass-and-steel structure eighty metres high, envisioned as a combination of Kew Gardens and the Eifel Tower. It will serve as a continuation of the International Pavilion and a dispersal point for people going to the park and hotel on the north side of the development.

As always, the Deans paid meticulous attention to landscaping, especially the pathways. The bridge is reached from Sydney city centre through the serpentine covered passage which contains a walkway, closed circuit monorail and cycle path, shops and an open market. This blue snake is both eye catching from the outside and a dramatic, intriguing shape to travel through, and it solves the design difficulties posed by the straight line of the access route from Sydney to the bridge and across.

Another and much larger problem was presented by the proposed flyover—up to twelve lanes at its widest point—

linking the city with nearby Sydney Bridge. "It casts a giant shadow over the project," says Roger. "We are raising the land around it and planting trees. On the sunny side we are putting walkways around it. So we are attempting both to use and to disguise the flyover."

On the other side of the flyover from the harbour are the marshalling yards, built on reclaimed marshland with a small river running through it. The proposal is to create a large lake, dotted with island restaurants, structures for an educational theme park and, on the edge of the water, a hotel. Decorative green detailing and terra-cotta tiles on the buildings will give the area a Mediterranean feel, enhanced by the shape of the trees. Overlooking the whole fantastic scene will be office towers like illuminated sculptures of smoke billowing into the sky.

All this is a far cry from the Bauhaus Box and "machines for living." The chasm between the two styles is one of scale as well as kind. Functionalism is a catch-all dogma that has literally changed the face of Europe. All the projects here described and all those they might spawn would only ever represent a minute fraction of the buildings of the future.

Man, Roger Dean believes, is at odds with his habitat, the "dark, satanic mills" are an aberration; but the times are changing and they are on his side. It is already a commonplace to predict that the microchip revolution will affect everybody's life in the coming decades. More and more people will work, learn and shop at home on personal computers. Word processors and the rapidly advancing information technology will eradicate whole areas of employment, drastically cutting staffing levels and the size of offices. Yet, in spite of these obvious trends, the big property investors—the pension funds, mainly—are still planning as their next top-priority development, yes, the prestige office block.

Roger Dean believes that the future place of business will be centres providing conference, exhibition, shopping, entertainment and hotel facilities, as exemplified by the NEC and Subud projects. He sees these complexes providing a new, life-giving focus to our ailing city centres.

The opportunity that this would present for the Dean treatment, in architecture and landscaping, is clear. He points out: "If Disneyland was such a wonderful creation, it would be a city centre somewhere—it isn't. It is an amazing feat of imagination, but it does look plastic."

The lives of millions of city dwellers are plagued by mental pollution: the oppressive business architecture of the concrete jungle, the noise and stench of traffic. The standard of their lives, Roger Dean says, could be improved dramatically by re-creating a pleasant, interesting environment. A great deal of money is spent in pursuit of living in the right place; with the same money and a little imagination everywhere could be made the right place.

Despatch the fume-laden traffic to unseen roads under buildings, tear down the Glass Boxes, and choreograph new landscapes and architecture to delight and entertain the human beings that must live and breathe among them. Even if this were done in small, isolated areas, it would help, however slightly, to transform our cities from "machines for living" to living worlds. It would be a small step out of the shadow.